Geopolitical Chess

The West's Desperation And Russia's Strategic Response

GEW Intelligence Unit

Global East-West

Hichem Karoui (Editor)

Contents

Chapter One

The New Cold War: Origins and Overview

The re-emergence of tension between major global powers signals the advent of a modern Cold War, characterized by complex geopolitical rivalries and strategic maneuvering. This phenomenon, distinct from its historical predecessor, reflects the evolving dynamics of international relations in the contemporary era. As the world witnesses the resurgence of conflicts and confrontations, the concept of a new Cold War serves as a framework for understanding the intricate web of hostilities, alliances, and ideological schisms that define the global landscape. At its core, the modern Cold War highlights the intersection of traditional power struggles with novel dimensions of competition, including technological prowess, economic interdependence, and cultural influence. Understanding this paradigm shift is essential in comprehending the diverse challenges posed by world affairs. By delving into the origins and intricacies of this emergent dynamic, we can gain valuable insights into the forces shaping the international order and the potential pathways for navigating through this era of heightened tensions and rivalries.

Defining the Modern Cold War

The term 'Cold War' historically evokes the period of geopolitical tension and rivalry between the United States and the Soviet Union following World War II. However, in the modern context, the term has evolved to encompass a new era of global power struggles characterized by competition, brinkmanship, and ideological clashes among major players on the international stage. The modern Cold War is not confined to a single ideological divide but rather involves multiple actors with diverse agendas competing for influence, resources, and dominance. In this context, the term 'cold' does not denote an absence of conflict but rather a strategic and indirect form of confrontation that extends beyond traditional military engagements. Economic coercion, cyber espionage, propaganda campaigns, and proxy conflicts define the landscape of the modern Cold War. Unlike its predecessor, the modern Cold War is not defined by two opposing blocs but rather by complex and fluid alliances, often shifting based on strategic interests and regional dynamics. In some senses, the modern Cold War represents a clash between the forces of globalization and the desire for regional or national autonomy. It encompasses struggles for technological superiority, control of energy resources, and influence over emerging markets, making it a multi-faceted and intricate web of power dynamics. At its core, the modern Cold War reflects a battle for supremacy in a rapidly changing global order, where traditional notions of statecraft, diplomacy, and warfare are being redefined. Understanding the nuances of this modern contest is crucial for grasping the complexities of contemporary international relations and the potential trajectory of global stability and security.

Key Actors and Their Interests

The modern Cold War is characterized by the involvement of various key actors, each with their own complex set of interests and priorities. At the forefront of this global geopolitical landscape are the United States and Russia, whose historical rivalry and contrasting ideological frameworks have underpinned much of the tension and competition witnessed in recent years. Both nations seek to maintain and expand their spheres of influence, with Russia aiming to assert dominance over its immediate neighboring states and the U.S. striving to uphold its global leadership position.

China, as a rising superpower, has also emerged as a critical player in this new Cold War paradigm. With its expanding economic prowess and ambitious One Belt One Road initiative, China seeks to solidify its position as a dominant force in international affairs, challenging the traditional Western-centric power structure. Additionally, regional powers such as Iran, North Korea, and Turkey have become influential actors, often leveraging their strategic positioning to advance their respective agendas while impacting the broader Cold War dynamics.

The European Union and NATO member states play a pivotal role in shaping the contours of the modern Cold War. As transatlantic alliances face internal strains and external pressures, the strategic interests and security concerns of these entities significantly impact the overall geopolitical landscape. Moreover, non-state actors, including multinational corporations, non-governmental organizations, and transnational extremist groups, exert influence in ways that complicate the traditional state-centric framework of international politics.

Beyond nation-states, the field of information warfare and cyber capabilities has elevated the significance of non-traditional actors, with technological advancements enabling sophisticated cyber-attacks, disinformation campaigns, and subversive activities. The proliferation of state-sponsored and independent hacking groups has further blurred the lines between conventional and unconventional actors in shaping the global balance of power.

The intersection of national interests, regional dynamics, and global ambitions underscores the multifaceted nature of the contemporary Cold War landscape. As these key actors navigate the complexities of power projection, strategic maneuvering, and ideological conflicts, the resulting interplay continues to define the parameters of international relations and shape the trajectory of future geopolitical developments.

Geopolitical Triggers and Flashpoints

The escalation of geopolitical triggers and the emergence of flashpoints have become defining features of the contemporary new Cold War. Geopolitical triggers signify events or actions that precipitate tension between nations, often rooted in conflicting strategic interests or territorial disputes. These triggers can range from military exercises near disputed borders to provocative diplomatic gestures that challenge the status quo. As such triggers provoke responses from opposing powers, they contribute to the amplification of international tensions and the crystallization of an adversarial climate. Flashpoints, on the other hand, denote specific geographic locations or issues that serve as focal points for conflict and potential escalation. These can include contested territories, vital trade routes, or regions where historical animosities and power dynamics converge. The strategic significance of these flashpoints often magnifies their impact on global stability and security. Addressing these geopolitical triggers and flashpoints requires a nuanced understanding of historical contexts, national interests, and the complex interplay of military, economic, and diplomatic factors. Key aspects to consider encompass the role of regional alliances, the presence of external actors seeking to exert influence, and the potential for unintended consequences stemming from miscalculations. It is critical to assess how these triggers and flashpoints are utilized as instruments of statecraft and leverage by involved parties. Furthermore, the proliferation of technology has introduced novel dimensions to the persistence and exacerbation of geopolitical triggers and flashpoints. From cyber operations aimed at destabilizing adversaries to the militarization of outer space, technological advancements have redefined the traditional battlegrounds and expanded the spectrum of potential conflicts. The interconnectedness facilitated by digital infrastructure also introduces vulnerabilities and opportunities for disruption, intensifying the need for robust defense mechanisms and safeguards. As such, grappling with the intricacies of geopolitical triggers and flashpoints demands a comprehensive and multifaceted approach, underscored by meticulous analysis, proactive diplomacy, and the cultivation of constructive channels for dialogue. Ultimately, it is imperative to navigate this landscape with prudence, recognizing the far-reaching implications of each action and the imperative of averting a descent into protracted conflict.

Technological Advancements and Warfare

The intersection of technology and warfare has always been a critical aspect of global conflicts throughout history. The present era, marked by the resurgence of geopolitical tensions akin to the Cold War, is experiencing an unprecedented surge in technological advancements that have profound implications for modern warfare. From AI-driven autonomous weapons to the militarization of space, technological developments are reshaping the dynamics of conflict and defense strategies on a global scale.

One of the most influential advancements in contemporary warfare is the integration of artificial intelligence (AI) into military systems. AI-powered technologies are increasingly being deployed for autonomous reconnaissance, target identification, and even decision-making in combat scenarios. This raises complex ethical and strategic considerations as it shifts the traditional human-centric approach to warfare towards more automated and potentially unpredictable engagements. Moreover, the rapid evolution of AI introduces challenges in regulating and controlling autonomous weapons systems to ensure compliance with international laws and ethical standards.

Simultaneously, cyber warfare has emerged as a predominant domain in modern conflict. State-sponsored cyber-attacks and espionage have become pervasive tools in geopolitical confrontations, evidenced by high-profile incidents such as interference in electoral processes and large-scale data breaches. The interconnected nature of global networks and critical infrastructure amplifies the vulnerabilities to cyber threats, thereby necessitating robust cybersecurity measures and defensive capabilities. As digital interdependencies continue to deepen, the potential for devastating cyber warfare significantly escalates, posing substantial security risks to nations and their citizens.

Furthermore, the advent of hypersonic weapons represents a disruptive leap in military technology. These high-speed, maneuverable missiles can penetrate existing defense systems with unprecedented speed and agility, rendering traditional countermeasures insufficient. The development and deployment of hypersonic weapons by major powers underscore a renewed arms race and accentuate the complexity of strategic deterrence in an era defined by rapid technological innovation. Additionally, the militarization of outer space presents a new frontier for potential conflict and competition, fueling concerns about the peaceful use of space assets and satellite-based capabilities.

In conclusion, technological advancements in warfare profoundly impact the evolving landscape of global security and defense. As nations navigate the complexities of harnessing cutting-edge technologies within the framework of international law and ethical norms, the intersection of innovation and conflict redefines modern warfare's parameters.

Economic Tensions and Trade Conflicts

The realm of international relations is intrinsically linked to economic dimensions, and in the context of the new Cold War, the role of economic tensions and trade conflicts cannot be overlooked. Against the backdrop of geopolitical rivalries and diverging strategic interests, economic warfare has emerged as a central feature, wielding significant influence over the dynamics between major powers. The utilization of economic instruments as tools of statecraft has intensified, leading to complex and multifaceted trade conflicts that have reverberated across global markets. The contest for economic supremacy and dominance has unfolded through the imposition of tariffs, sanctions, and trade barriers, with each side leveraging its economic leverage to gain strategic advantages and assert influence. This has not only set the stage for direct economic confrontations but has also cascaded into broader ramifications, encompassing diverse sectors such as technology, finance, energy, and beyond. The interplay of economic interdependence and competition has engendered a web of complexities, shaping the contours of the new Cold War. Furthermore, the interconnected nature of the global economy has meant that trade conflicts and economic tensions have rippled beyond the primary actors, impacting allied and neutral nations and thereby contributing to a widening network of economic implications and consequences. In navigating these turbulent waters, policymakers and analysts are compelled to grapple with the intricate interlinkages between economic dynamics, security imperatives, and geopolitical strategies, recognizing the multi-layered nature of contemporary international relations. As the new Cold War continues to unfold, the management of economic tensions and trade conflicts stands as a pivotal challenge, requiring astute navigation, calibrated responses, and a keen understanding of the intricate interplay between economics and geopolitics.

Nuclear Deterrence and Arms Race Dynamics

Nuclear deterrence has remained a central pillar in the

complex web of international relations since the outset of the Cold War. The possession and deployment of nuclear weapons by global powers have exerted a profound influence on geopolitics, ushering in an era characterized by strategic tension and the specter of mutually assured destruction. The doctrine of deterrence operates on the premise that the threat of massive retaliation will dissuade adversaries from initiating a nuclear conflict, thereby maintaining a delicate equilibrium. This precarious balance has engendered a palpable sense of unease and trepidation, with the potential for catastrophic consequences looming large over the international community.

The arms race, a fundamental result of nuclear deterrence, has fueled the incessant pursuit of technological superiority and military dominance. Competing powers have endeavored to amass formidable arsenals, striving to outpace their rivals and solidify their strategic preeminence. This relentless quest for supremacy has precipitated a relentless cycle of weapon development, culminating in the proliferation of increasingly sophisticated and destructive capabilities. Such escalation engenders a climate of suspicion and mistrust, amplifying the stakes in the realm of national security and global stability.

Moreover, integrating emerging technologies into nuclear armaments has introduced unprecedented complexities into the dynamics of deterrence and the arms race. Advancements in cyber warfare and artificial intelligence have opened new frontiers for potential exploitation, presenting opportunities and vulnerabilities in nuclear defense strategies. The prospect of non-state actors acquiring or leveraging nuclear capabilities further underscores the imperative of proactive risk mitigation and robust deterrence mechanisms.

Multifaceted challenges and evolving paradigms mark the contemporary landscape of nuclear deterrence and the arms race. The resurgence of great power competition and asymmetrical threats and regional rivalries necessitates a holistic reevaluation of existing doctrines and policies. Striking a delicate equilibrium between preserving strategic stability and averting the perils of proliferation requires a judicious blend of diplomacy, vigilance, and resolute commitment to non-proliferation efforts. As the global community stands at the precipice of uncertain times, navigating the intricacies of nuclear deterrence and arms race dynamics demands collective introspection and concerted action to uphold peace and security on a global scale.

Alliances and International Relations

In today's complex geopolitical landscape, alliances and international relations play a pivotal role in shaping the dynamics of the new Cold War. Nations around the world are strategically aligning themselves with either the Western or Eastern bloc, seeking to secure their interests and influence global affairs. The traditional power structure of international relations is being tested and reshaped, leading to a delicate balance of alliances and strategic partnerships.

The NATO alliance stands as a cornerstone of Western defense and serves as a bulwark against potential aggression from adversarial forces. Its members, including the United States and several European nations, have committed to mutual defense and collective security, sending a strong message of unity and deterrence. On the other hand, Russia has sought to solidify alliances with countries that share its political and economic philosophies, forming crucial partnerships in regions such as Central Asia and the Middle East.

Beyond military alliances, economic and trade relations are also key components of international relations in the context of the new Cold War. The United States and its allies have employed sanctions and diplomatic pressure to isolate Russia economically and limit its global influence. Conversely, Russia has pursued closer economic ties with like-minded nations, attempting to bolster its position through energy partnerships and economic cooperation agreements.

Furthermore, the evolving nature of international relations in the digital age has introduced new complexities and challenges. Cybersecurity concerns have driven nations to collaborate on cyberdefense initiatives and information-sharing protocols. At the same time, accusations of cyberattacks and disinformation campaigns have strained relations between major powers, highlighting the intricate interplay between technological capabilities and international politics.

The United Nations and other multilateral forums continue to serve as platforms for dialogue and negotiation, offering opportunities for diplomacy and conflict resolution in the midst of escalating tensions. However, the diverging interests of major powers have tested the effectiveness of these institutions, raising questions about their ability to mitigate and manage conflicts in an era defined by renewed great power competition.

Ultimately, the intricate web of alliances and international relations reflects the multifaceted nature of the new Cold War, underscoring the interdependence of nations and the far-reaching implications of their strategic choices. As the global order continues to evolve, the dynamics of international relations will remain a critical factor in shaping the trajectory of this unprecedented era of geopolitical confrontation.

Cultural and Ideological Divides

Cultural and ideological divides serve as the undercurrents shaping the immense power play in the New Cold War. The clash between worldviews, value systems, and belief structures significantly influences the behavior and policies of global actors. At the heart of this divide are contrasting interpretations of freedom, governance, individual rights, and societal aspirations. These disparities have manifested in a multitude of ways, reverberating across international relations, economic strategies, military alliances, and diplomatic negotiations.

The cultural dimensions of this schism are multifaceted, permeating through art, literature, education, and popular culture. Different societies embrace distinct artistic expressions, literary traditions, and educational paradigms, often reflecting divergent historical narratives and national identities. These nuanced distinctions create lenses through which nations perceive themselves and others, influencing their interactions with the external world. Moreover, they fuel narratives of exceptionalism and superiority that can exacerbate geopolitical tensions.

Moreover, the ideological rift is characterized by competing political systems, governing principles, and socio-economic models. The clash between liberal democracies, autocratic regimes, and hybrid systems has become increasingly pronounced, shaping global debates on human rights, sovereignty, and global governance. The quest for ideological hegemony has amplified competition over institutions, norms, and regional spheres of influence. This ideological struggle extends to economic ideologies, technocratic approaches, and visions of sustainable development, generating friction in trade relations, investment practices, and multilateral cooperation.

Religious, philosophical, and ethical disparities further augment the cultural and ideological schism. Varying religious beliefs, secular philosophies, and ethical frameworks underpin diverse perceptions of morality, justice, and existential purpose. These disparities are susceptible to manipulation and exploitation, often becoming fault lines for identity-based conflicts and radicalization, perpetuating animosity and mistrust among nations.

Bridging these divides necessitates holistic engagement, mutual understanding, and reciprocal respect. Efforts to transcend cultural and ideological barriers demand dialogue, empathy, and the cultivation of shared spaces for exchange and collaboration. Acknowledging the complexity and legitimacy of diverse perspectives can enable the construction of durable bridges across chasms of difference, fostering a more harmonious and interconnected global landscape.

Summary and Transition into Historical Context

The cultural and ideological divides have played a significant role in shaping the landscape of the new Cold War. These divides are deeply rooted in historical narratives, political ideologies, and societal values that are unique to each major player in this global power struggle. As we transition from this exploration into the historical context, it's crucial to underscore the profound impact of cultural and ideological differences on international relations. The clash of values, belief systems, and national identities has fueled political tensions and seeped into economic, military, and diplomatic arenas. One cannot overlook the complexity and intricacy of these divides, exacerbated by the resurgence of nationalism, the proliferation of information warfare, and the erosion of trust in multilateral institutions. It is imperative to delve into these divisions' historical roots to understand the current state of affairs comprehensively. By tracing back the historical trajectories of major geopolitical powers, we can discern the legacies of past conflicts, alliances, and strategic ambitions that continue to shape contemporary policies and attitudes. This historical lens provides crucial insights into the enduring nature of geopolitical rivalries and their far-reaching implications. Moreover, it allows us to appreciate the interconnectedness of past events with present-day dynamics, shedding light on the recurring patterns and evolving strategies employed by nations embroiled in this new Cold War. From the ideological standoffs of the Cold War era to the socio-cultural upheavals of the 21st century, the historical context offers a tapestry of narratives, turning points, and pivotal moments that have set the stage for the current global standoff. Examining the historical lineage of cultural and ideological fault lines grants us the capacity to discern the underlying motivations, fears, and ambitions that drive the actions and reactions of contemporary state actors. As we pivot towards a historical perspective, it becomes evident that the new Cold War is not solely a product of recent events; rather, it is deeply intertwined with the complex legacies of past confrontations, revolutions, and treaty arrangements. Understanding this intricate interplay between history and the present is pivotal in navigating the complexities of the new Cold War and devising informed strategies to mitigate its risks and repercussions.

Chapter Two

Historical Backdrop: From Allies to Adversaries

The Shifting Sands of Geopolitics

The intricacies of global geopolitics are akin to the intricate dance of shifting tectonic plates, constantly creating and redefining the landscape of international relations. Throughout modern history, the world has witnessed a dynamic interplay of alliances and allegiances that have remarkably shaped our current geopolitical terrain. From the tumultuous aftermath of World War II to the present era of complex power dynamics, these fluctuations in global political alliances have significantly impacted the current state of international relations.

At the heart of this intricate tapestry lies the seismic events of World War II, which not only altered the physical boundaries of nations but also reshaped geopolitical relationships on an unprecedented scale. The convergence of forces aligned against a common enemy laid the groundwork for remarkable alliances founded upon shared objectives and mutual support. The seeds of co-operation sown amidst the flames of war ushered in an era of geopolitical realignment and redefined the very fabric of global power structures.

However, this period of seemingly unified purpose was not immune to the underlying complexities and diverging ideologies that laid the groundwork for future discord. As the dust settled on the battlefield, the chasms of differing political systems and philosophical underpinnings emerged as fault lines that would come to define the post-war era. The ideological schism between the Western capitalist bloc and the Eastern communist bloc set the stage for a protracted struggle, casting a pervasive shadow over the geopolitical landscape and laying the foundation for the formation of enduring rivalries and alliances.

The ebbs and flows of ideological confrontation and détente have sculpted the contours of the global arena, giving rise to pivotal historical junctures such as the Cuban Missile Crisis and the proxy wars that exemplified the tensions between superpower blocs. These seminal events stand as testaments to the enduring impact of geopolitical shifts and their role in defining the geopolitical fault lines that shape our contemporary reality.

As we navigate the complex maze of current geopolitical

tensions, it becomes increasingly imperative to trace the historical trajectory that has led us to our present circumstances. By unraveling the narrative of shifting geopolitical sands, we can gain invaluable insights into the forces that continue to mold and reshape our geopolitical realities, offering a nuanced understanding of the intricate interplay between global alliances and the relentless tides of geopolitical change.

World War II Cooperation: Seeds of Alliance

World War II was a defining period in global history, where the tides of geopolitical alliances were tested and transformed. The seeds of alliance between the United States, the United Kingdom, and the Soviet Union were sown amidst the tumultuous backdrop of war. Prior to the outbreak of hostilities, geopolitical dynamics had been shaped by evolving power structures and ideological clashes, setting the stage for the cooperation that would define the war effort. As the Axis powers, led by Germany, Italy, and Japan, sought to expand their influence, the democratic nations found themselves united by a common cause. Recognizing the threat posed by totalitarian aggression, these nations set aside their differences and banded together in the fight against tyranny. The Lend-Lease program, through which the U.S. provided military aid to allies, including the Soviet Union, exemplified the extent of this cooperation. This chapter will delve into the intricate web of economic, military, and political collaborations that underpinned this unprecedented coalition against a common foe. It will explore the strategic decisions and diplomatic negotiations that solidified the alliance, as well as the challenges and complexities inherent in such multinational cooperation. Moreover, it will illuminate the far-reaching impact of this era on the post-war world order, laying the foundation for the subsequent emergence of the Cold War. By understanding the roots of this alliance, we gain valuable insights into the complex interplay of interests and ideologies that continue to shape international relations to this day.

The Iron Curtain and the Emergence of the Cold War

Following the end of World War II, the once-solid alliance between the United States and the Soviet Union began to unravel as ideological and strategic differences came to the fore. The term 'Iron Curtain,' famously coined by Winston Churchill in 1946, vividly encapsulated the division that had descended across Europe, separating the communist Eastern bloc from the capitalist Western bloc. This symbolic divide marked the onset of a prolonged era of suspicion, hostility, and geopolitical maneuvering that would come to be known as the Cold War.

The post-war period witnessed the rapid emergence of two distinct spheres of influence. The United States championed democratic principles and free-market capitalism, while the Soviet Union sought to spread communism's reach and establish satellite states across Eastern Europe. As each superpower vied for dominance, tensions escalated, and the specter of nuclear conflict loomed large over the international stage.

At the heart of the emerging Cold War was a clash of ideologies, epitomized by the contrasting economic systems of capitalism and communism. The introduction of the Marshall Plan by the United States to aid the war-torn nations of Europe represented an apparent attempt to prevent the spread of communism by promoting economic recovery and stability. In response, the Soviet Union fostered its own sphere of influence and established the Cominform to consolidate control over communist parties in various countries, intensifying the ideological battleground.

The Berlin Airlift of 1948-1949, following the Soviet Union's blockade of West Berlin, served as a potent symbol of the ideological confrontation, demonstrating the resolve of the Western powers to defy Soviet coercion and protect the principles of democracy. Meanwhile, the establishment of NATO in 1949 and the subsequent formation of the Warsaw Pact by the Eastern Bloc solidified the military standoff, heightening the global divide and deepening the sense of enmity between the two camps.

As the Iron Curtain descended, espionage and intelligence operations became instrumental tools in the clandestine struggle for supremacy. The actions of intelligence agencies such as the CIA and the KGB underscored the covert dimensions of the Cold War, as both sides sought to gain strategic advantage through subterfuge, disinformation, and covert operations. The proliferation of proxy conflicts in Korea, Vietnam, and other regions further underscored the global scope of the ideological struggle, putting millions of lives at risk and perpetuating a climate of fear and uncertainty.

In conclusion, the period following World War II witnessed the rapid transformation of erstwhile allies into entrenched adversaries, marked by ideological strife, military brinkmanship, and systemic distrust. The Iron Curtain became an enduring symbol of the division between East and West, setting the stage for a protracted and tumultuous era of geopolitical rivalry that continues to shape global relations to this day.

Ideological Divides: Communism vs. Capi-

talism

The ideological conflict between communism and capitalism has been a defining feature of the global geopolitical landscape for much of the 20th century. At its core, this schism represents an economic divide and starkly contrasting visions of governance, individual rights, and societal structures. Communism, grounded in the teachings of Karl Marx, advocates for collective ownership of the means of production, aiming for an egalitarian society where wealth is distributed based on need. In contrast, capitalism, championed by figures such as Adam Smith, emphasizes private ownership, free markets, and individual enterprise as drivers of prosperity and progress. These divergent ideologies have underpinned political movements, fueled revolutions, and shaped the international order, influencing alliances and conflicts across continents. The Cold War era witnessed the global battle between these two systems, with the United States and its allies championing capitalism and free markets while the Soviet Union and its satellite states rallied around communism. The ideological clashes played out through proxy wars, espionage, propaganda campaigns, and competition for influence in Eastern Europe and Latin America regions. The collapse of the Soviet bloc seemed to herald the triumph of capitalism, as former communist states embraced market-oriented reforms and integrated into the global economy. However, the persistent resonance of socialist ideals, coupled with increasing disparities in wealth and power, has sparked renewed debates about the merits and shortcomings of both systems in the 21st century. While some argue that capitalism fosters innovation and prosperity, others point to its tendency to concentrate wealth and perpetuate inequality. Similarly, while communism espouses equality and social justice, critics highlight its historical record of authoritarianism and economic stagnation. The clash of these ideologies continues to shape contemporary dynamics, from trade disputes and economic policies to debates over individual liberties and government intervention. Understanding the complexities and nuances of these competing worldviews is essential for comprehending the enduring influence of these ideological divides on global affairs.

Decades of Tension: Key Incidents and Crises

The decades following the Second World War were fraught with tension and significant incidents that strained relations between the United States and the Soviet Union. One pivotal event was the Berlin Airlift in 1948-1949, where Western powers supplied West Berlin by air after the Soviet Union blockaded all ground routes.

This demonstrated the resolve of the Western Allies and the escalating hostility with the Soviet Union. The Korean War (1950-1953) marked another flashpoint, with the U.S. leading a UN coalition against North Korea, supported by China and the Soviet Union. The Cuban Missile Crisis of 1962 brought the world to the brink of nuclear war as the U.S. and the Soviet Union confronted each other over nuclear missiles placed in Cuba. Further exacerbating tensions, proxy wars in Vietnam, Afghanistan, and other regions became battlegrounds for ideological struggles, seeding further distrust and animosity. These incidents underscored the pervasive sense of competition and mistrust that defined the Cold War era. Throughout these years, international diplomacy and strategic maneuvering took center stage as both superpowers vied for influence and control in a global power struggle reverberating across continents. The build-up of nuclear arsenals, espionage activities, and technological advancements heightened the stakes, creating an atmosphere of perpetual unease. As key incidents and crises unfolded, the world watched anxiously, knowing that any misstep could lead to catastrophic consequences. In summary, the decades-long period of tension and confrontation between the U.S. and the Soviet Union is punctuated by a series of critical incidents and crises that progressively deepened the divisions and suspicions, shaping the course of international relations and laying the groundwork for future conflicts.

The Fall of the Soviet Union: A Momentary Thaw

The fall of the Soviet Union marked a significant turning point in international relations, particularly regarding the dynamics between the United States and Russia. As the Soviet empire crumbled in the early 1990s, there was a palpable sense of optimism and potential for improved diplomatic relations between the former adversaries. The dissolution of the Warsaw Pact and the subsequent collapse of the Soviet satellite states in Eastern Europe led to a period of rapid change and uncertainty. With the end of the Cold War, an opportunity emerged to redefine global power structures and reshape geopolitical alliances.

In the wake of these transformative events, the U.S.-Russia relationship experienced a brief period of detente characterized by significant arms control agreements, such as the Strategic Arms Reduction Treaty (START) and the Treaty on Conventional Armed Forces in Europe (CFE), which aimed to reduce nuclear and conventional weapons stockpiles. Additionally, there were collaborative efforts to address regional conflicts, with both countries supporting peacekeeping missions in various hotspots worldwide. This thaw in relations was evident in the constructive interactions between leaders like

Mikhail Gorbachev and George H.W. Bush and their successors.

However, this period of optimism was short-lived as tensions began to resurface due to complex factors such as domestic political dynamics within Russia, discord over NATO expansion, economic challenges, and lingering arms control issues. Moreover, the enlargement of NATO to include former Soviet bloc countries served as a critical flashpoint, prompting concerns in Moscow about encirclement and the erosion of its sphere of influence. The Baltic states' accession to NATO and the broader security architecture in Europe exacerbated Russian apprehensions, leading to a renewed sense of distrust and animosity in the U.S.-Russia relationship.

The aftermath of the Soviet Union's collapse also saw internal turmoil and economic hardship in Russia, contributing to a growing sense of disillusionment and insecurity among the populace. The reconfiguration of political power and the struggle for stability posed significant challenges for the newly formed Russian Federation. Furthermore, the proliferation of nationalist sentiment and the quest for a new identity added complexity to its external engagements. These complexities significantly influenced the trajectory of U.S.-Russia relations, setting the stage for the evolving dynamics that continue to shape global politics today.

The Expansion of NATO: A Renewed Stress

The expansion of the North Atlantic Treaty Organization (NATO) has been a topic of significant debate and contention, particularly concerning relations between Western powers and Russia. The process of NATO expansion, which began in the aftermath of the Cold War, has served as a flashpoint for renewed tensions and strategic reevaluations. As former Warsaw Pact countries sought to integrate with Western institutions and enhance their security, the expansion of NATO's membership and influence has provoked a strong reaction from Russia.

From a historical standpoint, NATO's expansion represented a departure from its original role as a collective defense alliance aimed at deterring Soviet aggression. Russia saw the inclusion of former Eastern Bloc nations and later Baltic states into the alliance as an encroachment on its sphere of influence and a violation of assurances given during earlier negotiations. This perceived betrayal fueled growing animosity and suspicion, reshaping the dynamics of European security.

The strategic implications of NATO enlargement have been far-reaching. While some view it as a necessary step to consolidate democratic values and promote stability in Europe, critics argue that it has only deepened the divide between East and West. The prospect of placing military infrastructure closer to Russian borders has exacerbated concerns over national security and intensified geopolitical rivalries, underscoring the complex interplay of interests and aspirations on both sides.

Moreover, NATO's expansion has not been confined to geographical boundaries alone; it has extended to include broader security commitments and operational activities. This shift has drawn criticism from Russian leaders, who perceive it as a means to project Western influence into regions traditionally considered within Moscow's sphere of influence, such as the Caucasus and Central Asia.

Additionally, the diverging approaches to regional conflicts, particularly in areas such as Ukraine and Georgia, have further strained relations between NATO members and Russia. The alliance's support for these countries' aspirations for closer ties to the West has collided with Russia's own visions of regional order and influence, escalating friction and intensifying contests for geopolitical dominance.

In conclusion, the expansion of NATO has undoubtedly contributed to renewed stress in international relations. It has become a focal point for geopolitical maneuvering and generated apprehension over the future trajectory of Euro-Atlantic security. Understanding the complexities surrounding this issue is paramount to navigating diplomatic challenges and mitigating the potential risks of heightened confrontations.

21st Century Realpolitik: Reset and Relapse

The dawn of the 21st century saw a modicum of hope for improved relations between the West and Russia. The early years after the fall of the Soviet Union offered glimpses of cooperation, with efforts to integrate Russia into the global community as a partner rather than an adversary. However, this period of optimism was short-lived as realpolitik and geopolitical ambitions once again took center stage. The quest for dominance and strategic positioning led to a relationship relapse, marking a return to Cold War dynamics. The encroachment of NATO into territories once within Russian influence, combined with the expansion of Western influence through initiatives such as the European Union's Eastern Partnership program, sowed the seeds of resentment and suspicion. The Kosovo War and the 2008 Russo-Georgian War underscored the fragility of post-Soviet stability and signified the resurgence of power politics on a global scale. This period witnessed a rising tide of assertiveness from both sides as they sought to secure their interests in an increasingly multipolar world. The struggle for control over energy resources, particularly natural gas pipelines, became a focal point of contention, further complicating an already strained relationship. Furthermore, divergent perspectives on interventionism and regime change in conflicts such as Libya and Syria deepened the rift between former allies. The annexation of Crimea in 2014 and the subsequent conflict in Eastern Ukraine unleashed a new wave of tension, serving as a stark reminder of the enduring legacy of historical grievances and unresolved power struggles. The intricate web of economic interdependence intertwined with geopolitical maneuvering set the stage for a complex interplay of competition and cooperation, where strategic interests often trumped aspirations for global unity. The era of reset attempts and fleeting detente gave way to a harsh reality characterized by renewed antagonism, prompting a reevaluation of the nature of the contemporary international order. As the world grapples with balancing power and preserving peace, 21st-century realpolitik necessitates a sober understanding of the competing narratives and strategic calculations shaping the dynamic interaction between the East and the West.

Current State of Relations: From Cooperation to Competition

The current state of relations between the United States and Russia is emblematic of a complex history characterized by shifts from cooperation to competition. The 21st century witnessed both attempts at a diplomatic reset and a relapse into contention, exemplifying the multifaceted dynamics underpinning this geopolitical relationship. From the post-Cold War era to the present day, the interplay of global politics, security concerns, economic interests, and ideological differences has shaped this intricate dance between former allies turned adversaries.

At the turn of the century, hopes were high for a potential recalibration of US-Russia relations, as demonstrated by initiatives like the Obama administration's 'reset' policy. However, unresolved territorial disputes, conflicting approaches to regional conflicts, and diverging stances on critical issues such as missile defense and human rights led to a gradual souring of this renewed engagement. This was further compounded by the annexation of Crimea and subsequent hostilities in Eastern Ukraine, sparking a new era of tension and mistrust.

Today, the relationship finds itself ensnared in a web of strategic competition across various domains. Geopolitically, both nations vie for influence in regions such as Eastern Europe, the Middle East, and the Arctic, often clashing over spheres of influence and divergent foreign policy objectives. Militarily, arms races and modernization efforts reflect a resurgent focus on military capabilities and deterrence strategies, perpetuating a cycle of mutual suspicion and strategic posturing.

Economically, sanctions and trade restrictions have become tools of contention, impacting global markets and amplifying the overarching struggle for economic dominance. The confrontation in the cyber domain adds another layer of complexity, with accusations of state-sponsored cyber espionage and cyberattacks fueling an invisible war that operates beyond traditional battlegrounds.

The tit-for-tat expulsion of diplomats, propaganda warfare, and the weaponization of information further illustrate the multifaceted nature of this rivalry. Despite occasional attempts at dialogue and cooperation on specific issues, the prevailing narrative is one of adversarial relations marked by deep-seated distrust and antagonism.

As the US-Russia relationship continues to evolve, navigating the delicate balance between cooperation and competition remains paramount. Understanding the intricate interplay of historical grievances, contemporary challenges, and future possibilities is essential in formulating effective policies and strategies that transcend this enduring geopolitical tug-of-war.

Conclusion: Understanding the Past, An-

ticipating the Future

As we reflect on the historical backdrop that has shaped the current state of relations between nations, it becomes evident that the journey from cooperation to competition has been multifaceted and deeply influenced by a complex interplay of geopolitical, ideological, and strategic factors. The evolution of this relationship from allies to adversaries has been marked by pivotal moments that have left an indelible imprint on global history and continue to resonate in contemporary international affairs. Understanding this past is essential as we look forward to anticipating the future trajectory of these interactions. The tumultuous transition from collaboration to contention can be attributed to a confluence of forces that have reshaped the global order, compelling nations to recalibrate their diplomatic, economic, and military strategies in response to evolving threats and opportunities. As we grapple with the intricacies of this transformation, it is imperative to acknowledge the enduring legacy of past alliances and confrontations in shaping the lenses through which nations view one another today. Moreover, the conclusion drawn from a retrospective analysis underscores the need for nuanced foresight when envisioning the future dynamics between erstwhile allies turned adversaries. Anticipating the paths that lie ahead necessitates a comprehensive assessment of historical patterns, trends, and tipping points, as well as an astute comprehension of present-day power dynamics and emerging geopolitical fault lines. Furthermore, as we seek to prepare for the uncertainties and challenges that await us, it is incumbent upon leaders, policymakers, and scholars to critically evaluate the lessons learned from the historical continuum of cooperation and competition. This introspective examination can serve as a compass to guide our approach towards navigating the evolving landscape of international relations in an increasingly interconnected and volatile world. Ultimately, the culmination of understanding the past and anticipating the future demands a judicious balance of vigilance, strategic foresight, and deft diplomacy as global actors endeavor to steer the course toward constructive engagement, conflict resolution, and the sustainable pursuit of mutual interests in an era fraught with complexity and ambiguity.

Chapter Three

The Ukraine Crisis: Catalyst of Conflict

The Ukraine Crisis

The Ukraine crisis stands as a pivotal moment in contemporary international relations and regional politics, with ramifications that extend far beyond Eastern Europe. At its core, the crisis represents a convergence of historical, geopolitical, and socio-economic factors, reshaping the dynamics of power and alliances on a global scale. As such, understanding the roots and dynamics of this crisis is imperative in comprehending the current state of international affairs. The collision of interests among Ukraine, Russia, and the West has illuminated the complex interplay of historical grievances, strategic imperatives, and conflicting aspirations for influence and security. Moreover, the crisis has underscored the enduring resonance of Cold War-era rivalries and alliances, rekindling tensions and prompting renewed efforts to define the post-Cold War order. The significance of the Ukraine crisis pervades beyond its immediate actors, reverberating across the international system as a litmus test for the resilience of multilateral institutions and principles. As competing visions of world order collide in the Ukrainian theater, the crisis encapsulates the contestation between an established paradigm and emergent challenges to the status quo, calling into question the norms and rules underpinning global governance. Thus, The Ukraine crisis serves as a crucible for examining the fault lines and planes that intersect in the contemporary arena of international relations, offering insights into the complexities and uncertainties that shape the geopolitical landscape. By delving into the intricacies of this crisis, one can discern the intricately woven tapestry of strategic maneuverings, ideological contests, and human aspirations that define the modern era, shedding light on the evolving nature of power and influence in an increasingly interconnected world.

Pre-Crisis Relations: Ukraine, Russia, and the West

The dynamics of pre-crisis relations between Ukraine, Russia, and the West are intricate and rooted in historical, geopolitical, and socio-economic complexities. Ukraine's journey from a Soviet republic to an independent state was emblematic of the shifting power dynamics following the collapse of the USSR. As Ukraine sought to define its national identity and chart its geopolitical course, it found itself at the crossroads of competing influences. The European Union (EU) and NATO's outreach towards Eastern Europe intersected with Russia's historical sphere of influence, setting the stage for a tug-of-war over Ukraine's orientation. The interplay between these forces laid the groundwork for the hostilities that amplified the Ukraine crisis.

Russia's historical ties to Ukraine run deep, with centuries of shared history, cultural exchange, and intertwined economic interests. Moscow has regarded Ukraine as part of its strategic backyard, viewing Western encroachment with suspicion and concern. From the Russian perspective, Ukraine's potential alignment with the EU and NATO posed a threat to its national security and exerted pressure on its regional dominance. The annexation of Crimea, an autonomous republic within Ukraine, was a manifestation of Russia's determination to safeguard its interests and assert its geopolitical relevance. Additionally, the historically significant port of Sevastopol, home to the Russian Black Sea Fleet, underscored the strategic importance of Crimea in Russia's military calculus.

Conversely, Ukraine's aspirations for closer integration with the West were driven by a desire for democratic reforms, economic modernization, and alignment with Euro-Atlantic values. The pro-European movement gained momentum within Ukraine, particularly following the Orange Revolution of 2004, reflecting the populace's yearning for closer ties with Europe. Ukraine's economic potential and strategic location made it an attractive partner for the EU and NATO, further complicating the regional power dynamics. However, deep-seated corruption, political instability, and Russia's persistent efforts to influence Ukrainian politics injected volatility into the country's trajectory and intensified the ideological and geopolitical fault lines.

The West, represented primarily by the EU and the United States, endeavored to foster stronger ties with Ukraine, envisioning a prosperous and stable democratic partner in the heart of Eastern Europe. This approach aimed to bolster democratic institutions, promote economic reforms, and integrate Ukraine into the broader European framework. However, divergent priorities, wavering commitments, and internal divisions limited the efficacy of Western engagement, leaving Ukraine stranded in a geopolitical limbo. Moreover, the failure to provide a clear path for Ukraine's Euro-Atlantic integration emboldened Russia and stoked the flames of discontent within Ukraine, setting the stage for the crisis that would ultimately erupt in a confluence of historical grievances, political aspirations, and external influence.

The Trigger Events: Euromaidan and Crimea's Annexation

The trigger events of the Ukraine crisis, namely the Euromaidan movement and Crimea's annexation, have significantly shaped the course of the conflict and its aftermath. The Euromaidan protests emerged in late 2013 as a response to then-President Yanukovych's decision to suspend the signing of an association agreement with the European Union, opting instead for closer ties with Russia. The movement quickly gained momentum, drawing widespread support from Ukrainians who sought closer integration with the West and greater economic opportunities. Amid escalating tensions, the protests turned into a broader anti-government movement, marked by calls for political reforms and an end to corruption.

The Ukrainian government's violent crackdown on the protestors further fueled public outrage and led to a dramatic shift in the country's political landscape. This pivotal moment not only deepened the divide between pro-European and pro-Russian factions within Ukraine but also heightened geopolitical tensions between Russia and the West. The confrontations at Maidan Nezalezhnosti, or Independence Square, symbolized the struggle for Ukraine's sovereignty and the aspirations for a more democratic future.

Subsequently, Crimea, a region with a significant Russian-speaking population and strategic military importance, became the center of a controversial power struggle. Following the ousting of President Yanukovych, pro-Russian forces, supported by Moscow, seized control of key government institutions in Crimea. Against a backdrop of escalating unrest, a referendum was hastily organized, resulting in Crimea's annexation by Russia in March 2014. This move drew international condemnation and triggered a series of punitive measures, including sanctions and diplomatic isolation of Russia.

The events surrounding the annexation of Crimea underscored the complexities of overlapping historical, ethnic, and security interests in the region. It reignited debates over self-determination, sovereignty, and the principles of international law, reshaping global perceptions of territorial integrity and the use of force. These watershed moments' repercussions continue reverberating across Eastern Europe, shaping the regional dynamics and influencing the strategies of major powers involved in the crisis.

International Responses to the Conflict

The Ukraine crisis, particularly the annexation of Crimea by Russia and the subsequent conflict in Eastern Ukraine, prompted significant international responses from various actors on the global stage. The European Union (EU) and the United States were among the most vocal in their condemnation of Russia's actions, and they swiftly imposed a series of sanctions targeting key sectors of the Russian economy. These measures aimed to exert economic pressure on Russia to dissuade further aggression and promote a peaceful resolution. Additionally, numerous Western countries, including the US, Canada, and several EU member states, provided financial and military assistance to Ukraine, demonstrating their support for the country's sovereignty and territorial integrity. On the diplomatic front, international organizations such as the United Nations, the Organization for Security and Co-operation in Europe (OSCE), and the Council of Europe actively engaged in efforts to mediate the conflict and facilitate dialogue between the parties involved. Furthermore, the crisis sparked a significant shift in NATO's strategic posture, leading to an increased focus on collective defense and deterrence measures in Eastern Europe. Several NATO member states, particularly those in close proximity to the conflict zone, bolstered their military presence and conducted joint exercises to reassure allies and signal resolve to potential adversaries. Meanwhile, non-aligned countries such as China and India sought to maintain a balanced position, emphasizing the importance of respecting international law and seeking a negotiated settlement while safeguarding their own geopolitical interests. The broader international community, including regional powers such as Turkey and Iran, expressed varying degrees of concern and engaged in diplomatic initiatives aimed at de-escalating tensions and promoting stability in the region. Overall, the international responses to the Ukraine crisis underscored the interconnectedness of global security dynamics and the imperative of collaborative efforts to address complex geopolitical challenges.

Economic Implications for Ukraine and Broader Europe

The Ukraine crisis has had profound economic implications not only for Ukraine itself but also for the broader European region. The conflict has disrupted trade, investment, and economic cooperation between Ukraine and its European neighbors. Ukraine's economy has faced significant challenges, including currency devaluation, inflation, and a decline in GDP growth. Furthermore, the country's infrastructure has suffered damage due to the conflict, impeding economic development and recovery efforts. These economic repercussions have had ripple effects on the stability and prosperity of the broader European region.

In addition to the direct economic impact on Ukraine, the crisis has also affected energy security and supply dynamics in Europe. Ukraine has historically been a crucial transit country for natural gas supplies from Russia to Europe. The instability in Ukraine has raised concerns about potential disruptions to energy transport, leading to uncertainties in energy markets and affecting both Ukraine and European countries reliant on these energy flows. This has prompted efforts to diversify energy sources and routes, enhancing the strategic significance of energy infrastructure projects in the region.

Moreover, the economic sanctions imposed by Western countries on Russia in response to its actions in Ukraine have contributed to a complex web of economic consequences. These sanctions have impacted various sectors, including finance, energy, and defense, and have influenced global trade dynamics. The interconnectedness of the global economy means that these economic shifts have reverberated across the European continent, influencing investment climates and business operations. Businesses in both Ukraine and Europe have had to navigate the challenges posed by these changes, which are affecting their growth prospects and financial stability.

On a macroeconomic level, the Ukraine crisis has shaped discussions around regional economic integration and collaboration. It has highlighted the interdependence of European economies and underscored the need for cooperative mechanisms to address geopolitical tensions and promote sustainable economic development. Efforts to stabilize Ukraine's economy and enhance its resilience have intersected with broader initiatives to foster economic connectivity and mitigate risks to regional stability. As such, the economic implications of the Ukraine crisis have spurred conversations and actions aimed at recalibrating economic strategies and frameworks to adapt to the evolving geopolitical landscape.

Military Escalations and Ceasefires

The Ukraine crisis has been marked by numerous military escalations and attempts at ceasefires, reflecting the complex and volatile nature of the conflict. The military confrontations between Ukrainian forces and separatist groups in Eastern Ukraine, supported by Russian military assistance, have led to significant casualties and destruction. The use of heavy artillery, tanks, and other advanced weaponry has further escalated the intensity of the conflict, resulting in widespread devastation of infrastructure and civilian areas.

As international pressure mounted to de-escalate the situation, multiple ceasefire agreements were brokered, including the Minsk Accords. However, these ceasefires have been repeatedly violated, undermining their effectiveness and prolonging the suffering of the affected populations. Both sides have accused each other of violating the agreed-upon truces, leading to a cycle of broken promises and renewed hostilities.

The deployment of peacekeeping forces and monitoring missions has been proposed as a means to enforce the ceasefires and create a conducive environment for a lasting resolution. However, reaching a consensus on the composition, mandate, and deployment of such forces has proven challenging due to the deep-rooted mistrust and conflicting interests among the involved parties.

Furthermore, the emergence of new frontlines and areas of contention has complicated the prospects for achieving sustainable ceasefires. The strategic significance of key locations, such as Donetsk and Luhansk, has led to fierce battles and resistance from both sides, making it difficult to establish enduring truces in these critical areas.

The protracted nature of the military escalations and ceasefires has not only taken a toll on the combatants but has also significantly impacted the lives of civilians caught in the crossfire. The humanitarian cost of these confrontations, coupled with the challenges in delivering aid to affected regions, underscores the urgent need for a comprehensive and lasting resolution to the conflict.

In conclusion, the dynamics of military escalations and ceasefires in the context of the Ukraine crisis underscore the multifaceted challenges faced in achieving sustainable peace and stability. Addressing the underlying grievances, ensuring compliance with ceasefire agreements, and providing meaningful guarantees for long-term security are essential components in charting a path towards a durable resolution to this protracted conflict.

Humanitarian Impact: Refugees and Civilian Sufferings

The Ukraine crisis has unleashed a profound humanitarian impact, leading to the displacement of thousands of civilians and causing immense suffering. As the conflict escalated, countless families found themselves caught in the crossfire, with their lives shattered by violence and instability. The scale of human displacement has been staggering, with Ukrainian citizens fleeing their homes in search of safety and shelter. The influx of refugees has placed significant strain on neighboring countries and international aid organizations, challenging their capacity to provide essential resources and support. Among the most vulnerable groups affected are women, children, and the elderly, who have endured great hardship and trauma as a result of the crisis.

The human toll of the conflict extends beyond physical displacement, encompassing psychological and emotional scars that may take years to heal. Many individuals have witnessed and experienced harrowing events, leading to profound psychological distress and a sense of loss. Furthermore, the breakdown of essential services and infrastructure has exacerbated the plight of civilians, depriving them of access to healthcare, education, and livelihoods. The widespread disruption of daily life has sowed seeds of despair and uncertainty, leaving a deep and lasting impact on communities across Ukraine.

As the conflict rages on, humanitarian organizations are working tirelessly to address the urgent needs of those affected by the crisis. They are providing crucial aid such as food, water, and medical assistance, striving to alleviate the hardships faced by displaced populations. However, the ongoing hostilities and shifting frontlines present formidable challenges to delivering humanitarian relief, risking further escalation of the dire situation. Amid these challenges, the international community must rally together to ensure the protection and well-being of the innocent victims caught in the midst of conflict.

It is imperative to recognize that the repercussions of the Ukraine crisis extend far beyond its geopolitical dimensions; they reach into the heart of communities, where lives have been forever altered. While diplomatic efforts seek to resolve the political impasse, the pressing needs of refugees and civilians cannot be overlooked. By acknowledging and addressing the humanitarian impact of the conflict, we strive to uphold the values of compassion and solidarity, working towards a future where all individuals can live in peace and security.

Diplomatic Efforts and Peace Negotiations

Diplomatic efforts and peace negotiations have been integral in mitigating the Ukraine crisis and striving for a sustainable resolution. The international community, including key stakeholders such as the European Union (EU), United Nations (UN), and individual nation-states, has played a pivotal role in facilitating dialogue and mediation between the conflicting parties. Multilateral summits, diplomatic conferences, and peace forums have fostered constructive dialogue and sought consensus on crucial issues. Additionally, behind-the-scenes negotiations and shuttle diplomacy have been instrumental in bridging the trust deficit and narrowing down differences. Diplomatic envoys and mediators have worked tirelessly to explore common ground, build confidence, and pave the way for substantive negotiations. These diplomatic endeavors have demonstrated an unwavering commitment to finding peaceful solutions and preventing further escalation of hostilities. Addressing core concerns and grievances, recognizing the sovereignty and territorial integrity of all involved entities, and ensuring the well-being of affected populations have been central themes in the peace negotiations.

Balancing national interests with collective security objectives has required astute diplomatic finesse and adept conflict-resolution skills. Moreover, initiatives focusing on demilitarization, arms control, and confidence-building measures have been cornerstones of the peace negotiation process. Building on historical precedents and successful peace accords from other regional conflicts, diplomatic channels have leveraged effective strategies for fostering lasting reconciliation and stability. Amidst the complexity of geopolitical dynamics and entrenched animosities, sustained diplomatic efforts have reiterated the shared goal of establishing a durable and inclusive peace framework. The collective will and perseverance demonstrated in these peace negotiations must continue to guide the path toward comprehensive conflict resolution and sustainable peacebuilding.

Long-term Consequences for Regional Security

As we analyze the long-term consequences of the Ukraine crisis, it becomes evident that regional security dynamics have undergone significant shifts. The escalation of conflict in Ukraine has not only strained the relations between Russia, Ukraine, and the West but has also impacted the broader regional security landscape in Europe. The annexation of Crimea by Russia and the subsequent military intervention in Eastern Ukraine have raised concerns about the fundamental principles of territorial integrity and sovereignty, sparking apprehensions across neighboring countries. This has prompted a reevaluation of defense strategies and alliances, with several nations in the vicinity bolstering their military capabilities and seeking closer ties with NATO and the European Union to enhance their security posture. Furthermore, the ongoing turmoil has fueled apprehensions about the applicability and efficacy of international agreements and security frameworks, leading to renewed discussions on collective security measures and deterrent mechanisms. The persistent uncertainty stemming from the Ukraine crisis has prompted a reassessment of military doctrines and contingency planning, focusing on mitigating potential spillover effects and addressing vulnerabilities in the regional security architecture. Additionally, the protracted nature of the conflict has exacerbated societal divisions and ethno-national tensions, contributing to a climate of mistrust and animosity that may have enduring implications for stability and cooperation in the region. Beyond immediate security concerns, the Ukraine crisis has cast a shadow over the prospect of broader economic integration and development, as trade relations and investment patterns have been disrupted, raising questions about the sustainability of regional economic frameworks and partnerships. Moreover, the displacement of populations, internal displacement, and humanitarian crises resulting from the conflict have placed strains on social and political structures, potentially creating fertile ground for social unrest and radicalization. These multifaceted repercussions underscore the intricate interplay between security, politics, and socio-economic factors in shaping the long-term trajectory of regional stability and resilience. As stakeholders navigate the complex aftermath of the Ukraine crisis, it is imperative to adopt a comprehensive approach that addresses the interconnected dimensions of security, governance, and socio-economic well-being to lay the foundation for sustainable peace and prosperity in the region.

Conclusion and Transition to Russian Military Strategies

The long-term consequences of the Ukraine crisis for regional security are deeply significant and warrant a comprehensive understanding of the regional shifts in power dynamics, alliances, and military strategies. As this chapter draws to a close, it is essential to address the implications of these developments on Russia's future military strategies. The Ukraine crisis has led to a recalibration of Russia's military posture and approach to regional and global security. We must carefully analyze the evolving strategies employed by Russia as a result of the crisis and its impact on the broader geopolitical landscape.

Russian military strategies have notably transitioned in response to the Ukraine crisis. The annexation of Crimea and the ensuing conflict in eastern Ukraine have prompted a reevaluation of Russia's approach to military intervention and projection of power. In light of Western sanctions and diplomatic isolation, Russia has increasingly emphasized the modernization and expansion of its military capabilities, including advancements in cyber warfare, strategic missile systems, and unconventional warfare tactics. Furthermore, Russia has taken steps to fortify its military presence in regions adjacent to Ukraine, signaling an assertive stance that has reverberated across the international community.

Another crucial aspect of this transition is the integration of hybrid warfare tactics into Russia's military doctrines. The Ukraine crisis served as a testing ground for the application of hybrid warfare, which combines conventional military operations with information warfare, cyber attacks, and support for proxy forces. This approach has reshaped the nature of conflicts in the contemporary era and presents new challenges for security and defense strategies worldwide.

Considering the implications of these transitions, it becomes evident that the enduring legacy of the Ukraine crisis extends beyond regional boundaries. The evolving Russian military strategies have amplified security concerns among neighboring countries and have driven NATO and other international actors to adapt their own defense postures. The dynamic interplay between deterrence, escalation, and de-escalation strategies has become a focal point in the ongoing reassessment of security architectures within and beyond Europe.

Looking forward, an in-depth examination of the transition to Russian military strategies necessitates a nuanced understanding of the interplay between geopolitical ambitions, technological advancements, and diplomatic maneuvering. As such, the repercussions of the Ukraine crisis reverberate through the fabric of international relations, shaping the trajectory of conflicts, alliances, and strategic interests. It is imperative for policymakers, scholars, and practitioners to closely monitor and comprehend these transitions to inform informed decisions and cultivate sustainable frameworks for global stability and security.

Chapter Four

Military Posturing: Russia's Strategic Advances

Russia's Military Strategy

The evolution of Russia's military strategy since the post-Cold War era has been a significant concern for global security analysts. Following the collapse of the Soviet Union, Russia underwent a period of reevaluation and restructuring of its military capabilities and doctrines. This transition was marked by efforts to modernize and adapt to new geopolitical realities, leading to the development of a comprehensive military strategy that reflects the nation's ambitions on the world stage. Over the past few decades, Russia has demonstrated a notable shift in its approach to defense and security, drawing attention to its evolving military posture and tactics. Central to this transformation is the merging of traditional warfare principles with innovative technological advancements, shaping Russia's contemporary military strategy into a formidable force with both conventional and unconventional aspects. The country's emphasis on maintaining strategic deterrence capabilities through nuclear forces, combined with a focus on asymmetric warfare methods, has contributed to a complex and multi-dimensional military doctrine. Furthermore, the integration of cyber and information warfare components into Russia's military strategy has underscored the nation's commitment to leveraging non-traditional domains to achieve its security objectives. As such, the interconnectedness of various military elements within Russia's strategy underscores the need for a comprehensive analysis that delves into the multifaceted dimensions of its military planning and operations. Against the backdrop of shifting global power dynamics and regional conflicts, understanding Russia's military strategy is essential not only for diplomatic and defense communities but also for policymakers and scholars seeking insights into contemporary security challenges.

Recent Advances in Russian Military Technology

Over the past decade, Russia has made significant strides in modernizing its military technology, reflecting its commitment to enhancing its defense capabilities. The evolution of Russian military technology has been marked by a focus on innovation and adaptation to contemporary warfare challenges. One of the key areas where Russia has demonstrated advancement is developing next-generation combat systems, including advanced weaponry and sophisticated defense systems. For instance, deploying the S-400 surface-to-air missile system has showcased Russia's prowess in air defense technology, providing an extensive coverage range and exceptional performance against aerial threats. Moreover, introducing the T-14 Armata battle tank has further exemplified Russia's emphasis on cutting-edge armored warfare capabilities, integrating state-of-the-art features such as unmanned turrets and advanced armor protection. Expanding its drone fleet, encompassing a diverse range of unmanned aerial vehicles (UAVs), has bolstered Russia's reconnaissance and surveillance capabilities, enabling strategic intelligence gathering and operational support. Furthermore, Russia's investments in hypersonic missile technology have garnered considerable attention, with the successful testing and deployment of systems such as the Avangard hypersonic glide vehicle signaling a disruptive advancement in strategic missile capabilities. The development of these advanced technologies underscores Russia's formidable military modernization efforts and poses significant implications for global security dynamics. As Russia continues to refine and expand its military technological prowess, the evolving landscape of international security is increasingly influenced by the strategic implications of these advancements. It is imperative for the international community to closely monitor and assess the trajectory of Russian military technology as it shapes the broader context of geopolitical power dynamics and defense strategies.

Geopolitical Objectives Behind the Military Posturing

Russia's military posturing is deeply rooted in its geopolitical objectives, which play a pivotal role in shaping its strategic advancements and global influence. At the core of Russia's military posturing is the pursuit of reinforcing its status as a major world power and preserving its sphere of influence across key regions. By projecting military strength and presence, Russia aims to assert its role as a significant player in international affairs, particularly in areas historically considered within its sphere of interest. This includes regions such as Eastern Europe, Central Asia, and the Arctic, where Russia seeks to maintain strategic dominance and counter perceived encroachments by adversaries. Furthermore, the geopolitical objectives driving Russia's military posturing extend beyond mere defense and deterrence, encompassing an assertive stance aimed at reshaping global power dynamics and challenging the influence of Western powers. By maintaining a robust military posture, Russia aims to assert its presence as a counterbalance to Western hegemony, both regionally and globally. Additionally, Russian military assertiveness serves to safeguard its energy interests, transportation routes, and access to critical sea lanes, ensuring greater autonomy and leverage in global economic and security matters. Moreover, Russia's military posturing is inherently intertwined with its aspirations for political and diplomatic leverage on the world stage. Through strategic positioning and military prowess, Russia seeks to bolster its bargaining power in international negotiations, shape multilateral agreements in its favor, and project an image of strength and resilience to potential allies and adversaries alike. Overall, understanding the geopolitical objectives behind Russia's military posturing provides crucial insights into the intricate dynamics of global power struggles and the interplay between military strategy, diplomacy, and long-term national interests.

Key Military Installations and Their Strategic Importance

Russia's possession of key military installations across its territory and abroad plays a critical role in shaping its strategic posture and influence in global affairs. These installations, encompassing a diverse array of facilities ranging from air bases to missile defense systems, form the backbone of Russia's military capabilities and power projection. A detailed examination of these installations illuminates their substantial impact on regional security dynamics and international geopolitics. The significance of key military installations extends beyond purely defensive or deterrent functions to underpin Russia's broader geopolitical ambitions and capacity for coercive diplomacy.

One of the pivotal installations is the Severomorsk Naval Base, located on the Kola Peninsula. As the headquarters of the Russian Northern Fleet, this base holds immense strategic importance due to its proximity to the Arctic region and its claims over the valuable resources and shipping routes in the area. The base's access to the Barents Sea also provides Russia with a vital maritime gateway to the Atlantic Ocean, enabling it to project naval power and assert influence in the North Atlantic region. Furthermore, the strategic significance of the Tartus Naval Facility in Syria cannot be overstated. Serving as Russia's only Mediterranean naval base, it facilitates Moscow's sustained military presence in the region, allowing for expeditionary operations and serving as a crucial geopolitical lever in the Middle East.

In addition to its naval assets, Russia's extensive network of air bases constitutes a cornerstone of its military infrastructure. The Khmeimim Air Base in Syria, for instance, has emerged as a key operational hub for Russian air operations in the conflict-torn country, showcasing Moscow's ability to project air power beyond its borders and safeguard its interests in the region. Similarly, the deployment of advanced surface-to-air missile systems at locations such as the Hmeimim and Tartus bases demonstrates Russia's commitment to enhancing its integrated air defense capabilities, bolstering its deterrence posture in contested theaters.

The strategic importance of these military installations reverberates beyond their immediate operational functions, influencing regional power dynamics and fostering assertive postures in the face of perceived threats. As such, an in-depth analysis of these installations is essential to dissect Russia's strategic calculus and anticipate its military behaviors in various theaters of operation.

Russia's Approach to Naval Expansion

With its vast coastline and historical maritime ambitions, Russia has long demonstrated a keen interest in strengthening its naval capabilities. The country's approach to naval expansion involves a multifaceted strategy encompassing various elements, such as the modernization of existing fleets, the development of next-generation vessels, and the establishment of naval bases in strategic locations. The Baltic and Black Sea fleets play a significant role in safeguarding Russia's maritime interests and projecting power beyond its borders. Furthermore, the Arctic region has emerged as a critical theater for Russian naval expansion, driven by the melting of polar ice and the subsequent accessibility of lucrative resources and trade routes. As part of this expansion, Russia has been bolstering its presence in the Arctic by deploying advanced icebreakers and constructing new military installations. The strategic significance of these efforts extends beyond naval strength, with implications for economic, geopolitical, and environmental considerations on a global scale. Russia's naval expansion also intersects with its broader foreign policy objectives, as evidenced by the growing assertiveness in areas such as the Baltic Sea and the Mediterranean. Moreover, the ability to project power and protect sea lanes aligns with Russia's aspirations to assert itself as a formidable maritime player. This ambition is mirrored in developing sophisticated naval technologies, including submarines equipped with advanced stealth capabilities and long-range missiles, as well as the modernization of surface combatants. These advancements not only enhance Russia's defensive posture but also serve as instruments of deterrence and projection of influence. As the geopolitical landscape continues to evolve, the magnitude and implications of Russia's naval expansion will undoubtedly remain a subject of intense scrutiny and strategic assessment within international circles, influencing regional security dynamics and global maritime commerce.

The Role of Nuclear Capabilities in Deterrence

Nuclear capabilities have long been a central component of Russia's national defense strategy, playing a pivotal role in shaping global power dynamics and deterrence policies. The deployment and maintenance of nuclear weapons serve as a crucial element of Russia's military doctrine, serving to deter potential adversaries and safeguard national security interests. Within the context of international relations, the concept of mutually assured destruction (MAD) has heavily influenced how Russia perceives its nuclear arsenal as a credible deterrent against perceived threats. This ideology rests on the notion that any aggression towards Russia would result in catastrophic retaliation, thus deterring adversaries from engaging in hostile actions. Moreover, Russia's emphasis on maintaining a robust nuclear deterrent is rooted in the belief that it serves as a critical equalizer in asymmetrical power dynamics, particularly in the face of conventional military imbalances with the West. The strategic value placed on nuclear capabilities forms a cornerstone of Russia's military posturing, signaling its resolve to protect national sovereignty and interests on the global stage. Furthermore, the integration of nuclear weapons into military planning underscores Russia's commitment to ensuring strategic stability and preventing large-scale conflicts. As part of this deterrence strategy, Russia continuously modernizes its nuclear arsenal, investing in advanced technologies and delivery systems to bolster its deterrent capabilities. In recent years, the development of hypersonic missiles and other next-generation nuclear platforms has further solidified Russia's position as a formidable nuclear power. However, the reliance on nuclear deterrence also raises concerns about the potential risks and challenges associated with managing such a substantial nuclear arsenal. The intricate balance between deterrence and the risk of accidental escalation remains a critical consideration in Russia's strategic calculus. Moreover, the geopolitical implications of Russia's nuclear posture, including its impact on arms control agreements and global non-proliferation efforts, highlight the complex interplay of security dynamics at the international level. Consequently, understanding the multifaceted role of nuclear capabilities in Russia's deterrence strategy is integral to comprehending the broader implications of its military posturing and its influence on the evolving global security landscape.

Hybrid Warfare Tactics: Cyber and Information Warfare

In the realm of modern warfare, the term 'hybrid warfare' has gained significant prominence, reflecting the fusion of conventional military tactics with unconventional methods that exploit vulnerabilities in cyberspace and information networks. Russia's adept utilization of hybrid warfare tactics, particularly in the realms of cyber and information warfare, has raised considerable concern among Western powers and international security analysts. The combination of traditional military strategies with sophisticated cyber offensives and strategic disinformation campaigns presents a formidable challenge for adversaries. Cyber warfare encompasses a spectrum of activities, ranging from targeted intrusions into critical infrastructure to disseminating false narratives through social media and propaganda outlets.

Russia has demonstrated its proficiency in deploying state-sponsored hackers to infiltrate foreign networks, engage in espionage, disrupt essential services, and even launch large-scale cyberattacks with the potential to destabilize economies and societies. Furthermore, the orchestration of information warfare, including disseminating misleading narratives, manipulating public opinion, and exploiting divisive societal fault lines, has emerged as a potent tool in Russia's arsenal. This concerted effort to utilize disinformation to sow discord and undermine trust in democratic institutions underscores the evolving landscape of modern conflict.

The impact of hybrid warfare extends beyond conventional battlefields, permeating the digital domain and transcending geographical boundaries. The asymmetrical nature of cyber and information warfare confounds traditional military doctrines, compelling nations to recalibrate their defense strategies and invest in bolstering their resilience against these insidious threats. Collaboration among international allies, robust cybersecurity measures, and enhanced information literacy are imperative to effectively counter hybrid warfare tactics. Policymakers, military leaders, and technologists must remain vigilant and continually adapt to the dynamic challenges posed by hybrid warfare, recognizing that safeguarding national security in the 21st century necessitates comprehensive preparations in both physical and virtual domains.

Comparative Analysis with Western Military Strategies

The comparative analysis of Russian military strategies with those of the Western world reveals a complex interplay of capabilities, doctrines, and geopolitical considerations. One of the defining characteristics of Western military strategies is their emphasis on joint operations and integrated command structures. NATO, for instance, has developed a high degree of interoperability among its member states, enabling a rapid and coordinated response to various security challenges. In contrast, Russia's military doctrine significantly emphasizes centralized command and control, reflecting a more traditional approach to warfare. This distinction has important implications for the speed and flexibility of decision-making in times of crisis.

Another key difference lies in the respective approaches to technological innovation and modernization. While Western countries have invested heavily in areas such as cyber warfare, unmanned systems, and precision-guided munitions, Russia has sought to compensate for its technological shortcomings by focusing on asymmetric capabilities and hybrid warfare tactics. The integration of artificial intelligence and autonomous systems into military operations is also a notable divergence, with Western nations leading the way in this domain.

Furthermore, Western military strategies are underpinned by a commitment to transparency, adherence to international norms, and respect for human rights. NATO, for example, operates on the principles of collective defense and cooperative security, promoting stability and deterrence through dialogue and engagement. In contrast, Russia's military assertiveness in its neighboring regions has raised concerns about its willingness to challenge the established norms of international conduct, thereby contributing to heightened tensions.

Another aspect worth examining is the differing approaches to expeditionary operations and power projection. Western powers have extensive experience in conducting overseas interventions and sustaining prolonged military deployments, often in partnership with regional allies and global partners. In contrast, Russia's recent assertiveness in regions such as Crimea and Syria reflects a more opportunistic and calculated approach to power projection, characterized by a blend of conventional and unconventional tactics.

Moreover, using military force as a tool of diplomacy showcases a disparity between Russian and Western strategies. While NATO and other Western alliances place a strong emphasis on diplomatic resolutions and multilateral engagement, the Russian government has demonstrated a propensity to utilize military capabilities as a means of coercion and influence, often in tandem with information warfare campaigns.

In conclusion, the comparative analysis of Russian military strategies with those of the Western world illuminates contemporary global security's intricate dynamics. By recognizing the divergent approaches to command structures, technological innovation, adherence to international norms, power projection, and diplomatic engagement, policymakers and analysts gain crucial insights into the evolving landscape of international security and the potential for cooperation and competition.

Implications for Regional Security

The implications of Russia's military posturing are far-reaching and have significant repercussions for regional security. The enhanced military capabilities and assertive stance adopted by Russia have raised concerns among its neighboring countries and have reevaluated regional security dynamics. One of the key implications is the potential for heightened tensions and the increased risk of military conflicts in the region. Russia's demonstration of military strength, especially in Eastern Europe and the Baltic states, has generated unease and prompted these nations to seek reassurances from Western allies and international organizations. Additionally, expanding Russian naval capabilities and advanced military installations pose challenges to maritime security in the Baltic and Black Sea regions. This has increased patrols and surveillance activities by NATO and other allied forces, contributing to a more volatile security environment. Furthermore, the Arctic region's strategic significance has become the sharper focus as Russia continues to bolster its military presence there. The potential for resource competition and territorial disputes in the Arctic raises concerns about stability and cooperation in this vital area. Beyond the immediate vicinity, the ripple effects of Russia's military posture are felt in the broader European security landscape. The growing assertiveness of Russian military maneuvers has fueled debates about the adequacy of existing security arrangements and defense mechanisms. It has also prompted discussions on the need for renewed dialogue and cooperation between Russia and Western powers to mitigate the risk of miscalculation or escalation. Moreover, the implications extend to the global realm, as the interplay between Russia's military strategy and the response from major global powers reverberates across international relations. The region's evolving power dynamics and security challenges have necessitated a strategic reassessment by key stakeholders, including the United States, the European Union, and other influential actors. As such, the implications for regional security stemming from Russia's military posturing carry profound significance for the geopolitical landscape and demand careful consideration and proactive engagement to address the associated risks and uncertainties.

Conclusion and Future Perspectives on Russian Militarism

Russia's militarism has had far-reaching implications for regional security, making it imperative to analyze the potential future developments and their impact. As we look ahead, it is crucial to consider the multifaceted aspects of Russian military posturing and anticipate the evolving dynamics that may further shape global geopolitical landscapes. One key aspect of monitoring is the interplay between Russia's military advancements and the responses from neighboring countries and international alliances. The potential for arms races and heightened tensions in regions adjacent to Russia is a concerning prospect, and proactive diplomacy will be essential in mitigating the risks. Moreover, integrating cyber capabilities into Russian military strategies introduces new dimensions of conflict, necessitating robust defense mechanisms and collaborative efforts among nations to address emerging threats. It is also important to recognize the significance of public perception and propaganda in shaping the narrative around Russian militarism. Efforts to counter disinformation and promote transparency will foster mutual understanding and trust among nations. Looking to the future, the trajectory of Russian militarism will likely intersect with broader geopolitical shifts, including the evolving relationships between major powers and the impact of technological advancements on warfare. As such, comprehensive assessments of these trends and proactive dialogue among global stakeholders will be essential in shaping the trajectory of Russian militarism and its ramifications. By fostering greater cooperation and a commitment to peaceful resolutions, the international community can work towards reducing the risks associated with Russian militarism and pave the way for a more stable and secure global environment. At the same time, it is crucial to maintain vigilance and preparedness in addressing any potential escalation of military confrontations. Understanding the future perspectives on Russian militarism requires a nuanced approach considering political, economic, and technological dynamics. While challenges lie ahead, proactive engagement and strategic foresight can contribute to crafting a future where the impacts of Russian militarism are managed effectively and paths to constructive dialogue and collaboration are pursued.

Chapter Five

Economic Warfare: Sanctions and Their Global Impact

Economic Sanctions

Economic sanctions have long been employed as a tool of statecraft in international relations, serving as a means to modify the behavior of targeted nations or regimes by inflicting economic pain. These punitive measures are typically imposed to achieve specific foreign policy objectives, ranging from deterring aggression and destabilizing activities to addressing human rights violations and non-proliferation concerns. The fundamental concept underlying economic sanctions is the imposition of restrictions or penalties on a country's trade, financial transactions, or access to resources to induce change in its policies or behavior. Often presented as a peaceful alternative to military intervention, sanctions seek to exert pressure on target states in a bid to alter their conduct without resorting to armed conflict. As such, they represent a significant component of coercive diplomacy in the contemporary global landscape. A delicate balance exists between the intended impact of economic sanctions and their potential humanitarian consequences, which demands a nuanced understanding of the complex interplay between political will, economic leverage, and ethical considerations. Despite their contentious nature, economic sanctions continue to be part of the geopolitical toolbox, shaping the dynamics of interstate relations and offering both opportunities and challenges for international actors seeking to assert influence on the world stage.

Historical Context of Sanctions in Geopolitics

Throughout history, the use of economic sanctions as a tool of international diplomacy has been a defining feature of geopolitics. Economic sanctions can be traced back to ancient times when city-states and empires imposed embargoes and trade restrictions to exert influence and compel obedience from adversaries. However, during the modern era, economic sanctions truly emerged as a potent instrument of statecraft. The League of Nations employed economic measures against aggressor states in the interwar period, setting a precedent for using economic coercion to maintain international order and deter aggression.

The Cold War witnessed a proliferation of economic sanctions, with both the United States and the Soviet Union leveraging economic power to achieve their geopolitical objectives. The U.S. implemented trade embargoes and financial restrictions against communist regimes and their allies, while the Soviets utilized economic pressure to advance their interests in Eastern Europe and beyond. The collapse of the Soviet bloc did not diminish the utility of economic sanctions; instead, it marked the beginning of a new phase in the evolution of economic warfare.

In the post-Cold War era, the United Nations and individual nations have increasingly turned to economic sanctions as a non-military means of addressing threats to peace and security. The Gulf War of 1990-1991 saw a comprehensive embargo imposed on Iraq, while subsequent conflicts in the Balkans and Africa witnessed the targeted use of sanctions to coerce belligerent parties and bring about diplomatic resolutions. These experiences underscored the complex interplay between geopolitics, economic power, and the ethical considerations surrounding the imposition of sanctions.

Moreover, historical analyses reveal that the effectiveness of economic sanctions has varied widely, with outcomes ranging from regime change to prolonged suffering among civilian populations. Instances such as the failure of sanctions to alter the behavior of authoritarian regimes underscore the limitations and unintended consequences of relying solely on economic coercion. Concurrently, success stories, such as the diplomatic breakthrough with Iran, illustrate that well-calibrated and multilaterally-supported sanctions can incentivize policy changes and promote regional stability.

Ultimately, understanding the historical context of sanctions in geopolitics provides critical insights into the opportunities and challenges inherent in employing economic measures as a tool of statecraft. By examining past successes and failures, policymakers can refine their approaches to harnessing economic sanctions to promote international peace and security.

Types of Sanctions and Their Mechanisms

Sanctions are a critical tool in international relations, representing the economic arm of coercive diplomacy. Understanding the diverse forms and mechanisms of sanctions is essential for comprehending their full impact on targeted entities. There are several types of sanctions, each with distinct characteristics and operational strategies.

The first form of sanction is diplomatic sanctions, which involve reducing or severing diplomatic ties between the imposing state(s) and the target state, signaling disapproval and dissatisfaction with the latter's actions. These measures can include withdrawing ambassadors, suspending consular services, or limiting official communication channels. While not directly economic, diplomatic sanctions lay the groundwork for broader punitive actions and carry significant symbolic weight in the international community.

Another prevalent type is trade sanctions, often employed to restrict the flow of goods and services to or from the target state. Embargoes, quotas, and tariffs are common instruments used to impede trade as part of a coordinated effort to apply economic pressure. These measures aim to induce economic strain and compel policy change within the sanctioned nation by hindering the exchange of vital commodities and technology. However, it is crucial to consider potential spillover effects on global markets and the well-being of civilian populations when implementing such restrictions.

Financial sanctions represent a potent mechanism of coercion, leveraging the interconnected nature of the global financial system. This category encompasses asset freezes, capital controls, and restrictions on investment and credit, effectively isolating the target country from the international financial network. As modern economies heavily rely on financial flows and access to capital for stability and growth, these measures can exert profound strain on the sanctioned state's economic stability. Additionally, financial sanctions are designed to undermine the targeted regime's ability to fund its activities and projects, compelling internal reform or policy alteration.

Beyond these primary forms, there are also targeted sanctions, which pinpoint specific individuals, entities, or sectors within the sanctioned state for punitive action. This approach can be more nuanced and surgically precise, aiming to minimize collateral damage while applying pressure on key decision-makers and influential actors. This strategy maximizes the impact on the sanctioned entity by focusing on identifiable targets while mitigating adverse consequences for innocent civilians and neutral parties.

Supplementary measures encompass travel bans, arms embargoes, and technological restrictions, each wielding its unique influence on the sanctioned state. It's essential to recognize that effective sanctions utilize a combination of these mechanisms tailored to the circumstances and strategic objectives at hand. Understanding the intricacies and interplay of these various forms is integral to both policymakers' and stakeholders' grasp of the broader impact and implications of economic warfare through sanctions.

Assessing the Impact on the Russian Economy

Economic sanctions have undeniably played a pivotal role in shaping the trajectory of the Russian economy in recent years. To understand the extent of their impact, it is crucial to delve into the multifaceted dimensions of this influence. One significant aspect lies in the restrictions imposed on Russia's financial and energy sectors, diminishing its ability to access vital international markets and technologies. This has led to a ripple effect across various industries, with decreased foreign investments and technological advancements severely hindering growth prospects. Additionally, the devaluation of the ruble, prompted by the imposition of sanctions, has driven up inflation rates and eroded the purchasing power of Russian citizens, thereby presenting significant challenges for domestic consumption and economic stability.

Global Economic Repercussions

The global economic repercussions of the ongoing conflict between major powers are far-reaching and multifaceted. The economic warfare, particularly in the form of sanctions and trade restrictions imposed on Russia, has sent shockwaves across the world economy, impacting various sectors and regions. As one of the world's leading energy exporters, Russia plays a significant role in global energy markets, and any disruption to its production and export capabilities reverberates throughout the energy sector, affecting prices and supply dynamics. Furthermore, the interdependence of national economies means that any downturn in the Russian economy has ripple effects on international trade, investment, and financial systems. This has heightened the global concerns of businesses, investors, and financial institutions as they navigate the uncertainties and risks associated with geopolitical tensions and economic sanctions. The European Union, as a major trading partner with Russia, faces challenges in balancing economic interests with political considerations, leading to complex policy decisions and potential losses for businesses engaged in trade with Russia. Similarly, Asian countries, especially those with significant energy and commodity dependencies on Russia, are also closely monitoring the developments, mindful of the potential spillover effects on their own economies. Geopolitical tensions have manifested in currency fluctuations, stock market volatility, and supply chain disruptions, amplifying the global economy's interconnectedness. Moreover, sanctions and retaliatory measures have prompted trade patterns and investment shifts, reshaping economic relationships and alliances. Within this context of economic interconnectedness and interdependence, the repercussions of the ongoing conflict are felt deeply, underscoring the imperative for comprehensive analysis, strategic foresight, and collaborative policymaking to navigate the complexities of global economic repercussions amidst geopolitical turmoil.

Case Studies: Iran, North Korea, and Other Precedents

The utilization of economic sanctions as a foreign policy tool has been showcased through numerous case studies, with each providing valuable insights into their efficacy and broader implications. One notable case is Iran, where sanctions were imposed to curb the country's nuclear program. This led to significant economic strain, impacting various sectors, including energy, finance, and trade. The ensuing negotiations and eventual lifting of sanctions demonstrated the potential for diplomacy to ameliorate tensions. Similarly, North Korea has been subjected to stringent sanctions due to its nuclear ambitions and human rights violations. These measures have exposed the regime to severe economic isolation, prompting limited engagement with the global community.

Other precedents include the use of sanctions in response to human rights abuses, such as those enforced against certain individuals and entities. Additionally, targeted sanctions have been deployed against specific industries, aiming to disrupt revenue streams that support nefarious activities. In examining these case studies, it becomes evident that the effectiveness of sanctions often hinges on concerted multilateral efforts, highlighting the significance of international cooperation in shaping global responses.

Furthermore, the impact of sanctions extends beyond the intended geopolitical targets, permeating the wider global economic landscape. Adverse effects can be observed in interconnected markets and industries, underscoring the complex interplay between national and international interests. As such, a comprehensive understanding of historical precedents elucidates the multifaceted nature of economic warfare and its enduring ramifications.

In navigating these case studies, it becomes imperative to discern the nuanced challenges associated with imposing and enforcing sanctions. This necessitates a keen awareness of the intricate socio-economic dynamics within targeted nations, as well as a proactive approach to mitigate unintended humanitarian consequences. By delving into these historical examples, policymakers and strategists can glean invaluable lessons to inform future decision-making, emphasizing the imperative of employing sanctions judiciously and prudently in the pursuit of global stability and security.

Western Alliances and Responses

As economic warfare continues to shape the geopolitical landscape, the role of Western alliances in response to sanctions has become increasingly pivotal. The interconnectedness of economies and the need for collective action have underscored the importance of coordinated responses to mitigate the impact of economic measures. Western alliances, particularly those led by the United States and the European Union, have demonstrated a unified front in their approach to imposing and managing sanctions against adversarial states. These alliances have strategically leveraged their economic and political influence to garner broad international support for their initiatives. Through diplomatic channels and multilateral venues, Western powers have sought to build consensus among allied nations and gain adherence to imposed sanctions. This concerted effort has not only reinforced the collective strength of Western alliances but also exerted additional pressure on targeted states, amplifying the efficacy of economic measures. Furthermore, Western alliances have employed a range of innovative strategies to navigate evolving global dynamics, including engaging in dialogue with non-traditional partners to promote cooperative action. The growing emphasis on strategic collaboration and the pursuit of common objectives underline the resolve of Western alliances to uphold stability and confront destabilizing forces effectively. Concurrently, these alliances have devised mechanisms to cushion the impact of sanctions on their own economies, minimizing potential blowback and safeguarding mutual interests. While navigating the complexities of economic warfare, Western alliances have put forth a steadfast and coordinated front, signaling their unwavering commitment to upholding international norms and preserving global order. Moving forward, Western alliances face the ongoing challenge of balancing assertive policy prescriptions with maintaining diplomatic equilibrium. Striking a harmonious synergy between leveraging economic instruments and fostering diplomatic engagement will be critical in shaping the trajectory of future responses to economic warfare. As such, the cohesive actions of Western alliances in navigating the intricate web of economic sanctions will continue to play a defining role in influencing the dynamics of conflict and cooperation within the international arena.

Unintended Consequences of Economic Warfare

Economic warfare often waged through the implementation of sanctions, is a powerful tool in the arsenal of modern statecraft. However, its application is not without unintended consequences that can reverberate across global economic and geopolitical landscapes. One significant unintended consequence of economic warfare is the potential for collateral damage to innocent civilian populations. Sanctions imposed on a targeted state can lead to severe humanitarian crises, impacting access to essential goods and services such as food, medicine, and basic utilities. In effect, these measures can exacerbate suffering among the most vulnerable segments of society, undermining the moral authority of the sanctioning entities.

Furthermore, economic warfare can inadvertently stimulate the development of black markets and illicit networks within the targeted country as people seek alternative means to circumvent the restrictions imposed by sanctions. This informal economy can engender a culture of corruption and lawlessness, ultimately destabilizing the social fabric and perpetuating cycles of poverty and inequality.

Additionally, the imposition of economic sanctions can breed resentment and anti-Western sentiments among the populace of the targeted nation, potentially engendering a long-standing adversarial stance toward the sanctioning countries. This can perpetuate diplomatic tensions and hinder prospects for meaningful dialogue, impeding peaceful resolution. The erosion of trust and cooperation between nations can have enduring repercussions on international relations, impeding collaborative efforts on a myriad of global challenges.

Moreover, economic warfare may spill over beyond the targeted state, disrupting the global supply chain and inadvertently impacting businesses and industries in third-party countries. As interconnectedness characterizes the contemporary global economy, sanctions against a major player can lead to cascading economic disruptions with implications for trade, investment, and resource availability worldwide.

Understanding and mitigating these unintended consequences of economic warfare is integral to formulating responsible and ethical foreign policy. Policymakers must consider the broader social, economic, and geopolitical ramifications of their actions, seeking to minimize harm to civilians and prevent unintentional escalations of tension. Striking a balance between achieving strategic objectives and averting adverse humanitarian effects requires nuanced and thoughtful approaches to economic warfare in the 21st century.

The Future of Economic Sanctions as a Policy Tool

Economic sanctions have long been utilized as a tool of economic warfare and diplomacy, with the intent to curb or alter the behavior of target nations. However, given the evolving geopolitical landscape and global interdependencies, the efficacy and sustainability of economic sanctions as a policy tool have come under increased scrutiny. As we look to the future, it is imperative to critically assess the role of economic sanctions and their potential ramifications.

One of the central considerations lies in the unintended consequences of economic sanctions that extend beyond their intended targets. While the primary aim may be to pressure a specific regime, the collateral impact on civilian populations and the interconnected global economy cannot be overlooked. Furthermore, sanctions often lead to the emergence of illicit channels and black markets, undermining their effectiveness and exacerbating security challenges.

Another critical aspect is the reliance on unilateral versus multilateral imposition of sanctions. The effectiveness of economic sanctions is often contingent on broad international support and participation. In an increasingly multipolar world, garnering consensus and cooperation among diverse stakeholders becomes inherently challenging. Moreover, the coercive nature of sanctions can strain diplomatic relations and weaken collective efforts toward broader diplomatic solutions.

Furthermore, the rapid advancements in financial technologies and global trade patterns add layers of complexity to the enforceability and circumvention of sanctions. State and non-state actors have shown adeptness in leveraging alternative financial infrastructures and cryptocurrency platforms to mitigate the impact of traditional sanctions. This necessitates a reevaluation of enforcement mechanisms and strategies to ensure the efficacy of economic sanctions.

As we navigate the future of economic sanctions, exploring complementary or alternative policy instruments becomes essential. Diplomatic initiatives, humanitarian aid, and targeted engagement strategies can potentially offer more sustainable avenues for influencing state behavior while mitigating unintended humanitarian repercussions. Additionally, there is a growing emphasis on fostering inclusive, rules-based economic networks that offer viable alternatives to sanctioned entities, thereby incentivizing compliance and reform.

In conclusion, the future of economic sanctions hinges upon recalibrating their application within the context of broader geopolitical, economic, and technological dynamics. An informed and deliberative approach that considers the multifaceted implications of sanctions promotes multilateral engagement and explores synergistic policy measures will be pivotal in shaping a more effective and ethically sound framework for economic statecraft.

Conclusion and Strategic Insights

In concluding our exploration of economic warfare and its global impact, it is imperative to underscore the complexity and far-reaching implications of leveraging sanctions as a policy tool. The multifaceted nature of modern geopolitical relations necessitates a nuanced approach in evaluating the efficacy of economic sanctions, as well as their broader strategic implications. The use of economic coercion through targeted sanctions has become an integral component of statecraft, often serving as a means to influence the behavior of adversarial entities without resorting to direct military confrontation. However, the effectiveness of such measures remains contingent upon a multitude of variables, including the resilience of the targeted state, the alignment of international actors, and the interconnectedness of the global economy.

As we pivot towards the future, it is evident that the landscape of economic sanctions is continually evolving, prompting the need for recalibration and innovation in strategic policymaking. It is pivotal for policymakers and international stakeholders to adopt a comprehensive approach that considers short-term objectives and the long-term repercussions and unintended consequences of imposing economic penalties. The ethical dimensions of economic coercion also warrant careful consideration, particularly as sanctions may disproportionately impact civilian populations, leading to humanitarian crises that undermine global stability and security.

The strategic insights garnered from our analysis underscore the imperative of integrating economic tools with broader diplomatic and geopolitical strategies. Adhering to unilateral punitive measures may yield limited results; therefore, fostering multilateral alliances and consensus-building is paramount in maximizing the effectiveness of economic sanctions. Additionally, the harnessing of alternative instruments of influence, such as incentivizing positive behavioral change through diplomatic engagement and economic cooperation, could offer a complementary avenue for achieving desirable policy outcomes while mitigating the adverse fallout of punitive measures.

Amidst the prevailing geopolitical flux, it is discernible that the utilization of economic warfare demands a judicious balancing act, merging coercive actions with proactive initiatives aimed at de-escalation and conflict resolution. This necessitates a deeper understanding of the interconnected dynamics of international relations, coupled with astute diplomacy and strategic foresight. In essence, the future trajectory of economic sanctions hinges upon the adept orchestration of robust policy frameworks that uphold global stability, foster dialogue, and mitigate the collateral damage inflicted upon innocent civilians.

Chapter Six

Digital Warfare: Unseen Battlefronts

In contemporary conflict, digital warfare has emerged as a critical theater of operations, though often overlooked in traditional military analyses. This chapter aims to explore the profound impact of cyber and information warfare on the modern geopolitical landscape and examine the ways in which states and non-state actors leverage technology to achieve strategic objectives.

The digitization of military capabilities has transformed the nature of warfare, allowing for covert and asymmetric operations that can destabilize or undermine an adversary without the need for conventional kinetic force. Cyber warfare encompasses a wide range of offensive and defensive actions, including hacking, espionage, sabotage, and disinformation campaigns, all of which can potentially inflict significant harm on targeted systems and institutions.

Furthermore, the pervasiveness of social media and digital communication platforms has created new avenues for information warfare, disseminating propaganda, manipulating public opinion, and sowing societal discord both domestically and internationally. The weaponization of fake news, deepfakes, and social engineering techniques has redefined the battleground of ideas, posing significant challenges to democratic processes and public trust in institutions.

In this chapter, we will delve into case studies that illustrate the impact of digital warfare on geopolitical dynamics, such as the alleged Russian interference in the 2016 US presidential election and the cyber operations conducted during the ongoing conflict in Ukraine. We will also assess the evolving capabilities of state and non-state actors in the cyber domain, analyzing their tactics, techniques, and procedures to understand this unseen battlefront's complexities better.

Moreover, we will address the growing importance of cybersecurity and resilience in the face of digital threats, advocating for proactive measures to safeguard critical infrastructure, government networks, and private enterprises from malicious cyber activities. As the stakes of digital warfare continue to escalate, policymakers, military strategists, and technologists must collaborate in developing robust defenses and response strategies to mitigate the risks posed by this emerging domain of conflict.

As we probe deeper into the fabric of digital warfare, it

becomes evident that modern societies' interconnectedness amplifies the potential impact of cyber and information operations. Their reliance on networked systems for essential services, economic activities, and communication renders them vulnerable to sophisticated cyber-attacks, showcasing the need for continuous innovation in defensive capabilities and threat intelligence.

Furthermore, the proliferation of offensive cyber capabilities has ushered in a new era of geopolitical competition, wherein states invest heavily in developing offensive cyber tools to gain strategic advantage and project power in the digital domain. This shift has blurred the lines between traditional military operations and covert cyber activities, presenting significant challenges for international norms and legal frameworks governing state behavior in cyberspace.

The intersection of digital warfare and critical infrastructure introduces a realm of complex vulnerabilities, as demonstrated by the increasing frequency of cyber attacks targeting energy, transportation, and financial systems. The potential consequences of successful cyber intrusions in these domains could lead to widespread disruption, economic loss, and even endangerment of public safety, underscoring the urgency of bolstering cyber defenses across all sectors of society.

Moreover, as artificial intelligence and machine learning technologies continue to advance, the prospect of autonomous cyber weapons and intelligent malware introduces unprecedented dilemmas in attributing cyber attacks and discerning the intent of automated offensive actions. These developments raise profound ethical and legal considerations, necessitating international dialogue and collaboration to establish norms and regulations for the responsible use of advanced cyber capabilities.

In the realm of information warfare, the manipulation of online discourse and the dissemination of misinformation pose unique challenges to democratic governance, fostering societal polarization and eroding public trust in institutions. The proliferation of disinformation campaigns, tailored propaganda, and influence operations has highlighted the vulnerability of open societies to external influence and coordinated information manipulation, prompting calls for enhanced media literacy and proactive efforts to counter disinformation at its source.

Cyber warfare is not limited to attacks on traditional IT systems but also extends to the realm of critical infrastructure, where the potential consequences of successful cyber intrusions could lead to widespread disruption, economic loss, and even endangerment of public safety. The increasing digitization of essential services such as energy, transportation, and finance has made them lucrative targets for malicious cyber activities, highlighting the urgent need for comprehensive security measures across all sectors of society.

Furthermore, the proliferation of offensive cyber capabilities has ushered in a new era of geopolitical competition, wherein states invest heavily in developing offensive cyber tools to gain strategic advantage and project power in the digital domain. This shift has blurred the lines between traditional military operations and covert cyber activities, presenting significant challenges for international norms and legal frameworks governing state behavior in cyberspace.

The malicious use of artificial intelligence (AI) and machine learning in cyber operations presents a particularly insidious threat. AI can be employed to identify and exploit vulnerabilities in target systems rapidly, autonomously deploy malware, and adapt in real-time to defensive measures, making it increasingly difficult for traditional security measures to keep pace. As AI continues to advance, the potential for autonomous cyber weapons raises profound ethical and legal considerations, necessitating international dialogue and collaboration to establish norms and regulations for the responsible use of these advanced capabilities.

In information warfare, manipulating online discourse and disseminating misinformation pose unique challenges to democratic governance, fostering societal polarization and eroding public trust in institutions. The proliferation of disinformation campaigns, tailored propaganda, and influence operations has highlighted the vulnerability of open societies to external influence and coordinated information manipulation, prompting calls for enhanced media literacy and proactive efforts to counter disinformation at its source.

In conclusion, the multifaceted nature of digital warfare underscores the need for a holistic and integrated approach to cybersecurity, information operations, and strategic communications. By comprehensively addressing the challenges posed by cyber and information threats, we can fortify our defenses, uphold the integrity of democratic processes, and mitigate the risks of destabilizing conflicts in the digital age. Only through sustained vigilance, international cooperation, and technological innovation can we effectively navigate the complex landscape of digital warfare and preserve the stability and resilience of our interconnected world.

Chapter Seven

Political Plays: Leadership and Diplomacy in Turmoil

Political Dynamics

In the current landscape of international relations, the influence of political dynamics has been profoundly marked by turbulence and uncertainty. The decisions and actions of key global leaders have shaped diplomatic relations, triggering significant ripple effects on a scale that extends far beyond their immediate spheres of influence. This chapter delves into the intricate web of political interactions, examining the multifaceted nature of power play and decision-making within contemporary international politics.

The intricate interplay between national interests and global aspirations lies at the heart of these political dynamics. As leaders navigate the complex governance terrain, each strategic move carries implications reverberating across borders. Whether through assertive displays of military might, shrewd economic policies, or carefully crafted diplomatic initiatives, the choices made by influential figures can either inflame existing tensions or steer the trajectory of global relations toward stability and cooperation.

Moreover, the fragility of diplomatic equations is underscored by the inherent unpredictability of leadership decisions. In an era where the digital realm amplifies the reach and impact of every public statement or policy shift, the repercussions of political missteps are magnified, potentially escalating localized disputes into full-blown international crises. Consequently, the need for astute, sagacious leadership at the helm of nations and alliances becomes ever more pronounced as the implications of their actions resonate not only in the present but also for future generations.

Furthermore, the nuances of political dynamics extend beyond direct state-to-state interactions, encompassing intricacies such as the ideological alignments underpinning global organizations, the evolving role of non-state actors, and the impact of regional power struggles on broader geopolitical stability. As such, this chapter endeavors to unravel these interconnected threads, shedding light on the underlying currents that shape the political landscape and drive the direction of international affairs. Through a meticulous analysis of the influences at play and the decisions made at critical junctures, a comprehensive understanding of the intricate dance of political forces will emerge, providing invaluable insights into the complexities of contemporary global governance.

Profiles of Key Leaders

Understanding the personalities at the helm of nations is crucial as the geopolitical landscape undergoes rapid shifts and recalibrations. In this section, we delve into detailed profiles of key leaders whose decisions and actions have significantly influenced the course of the new Cold War. Understanding these individuals' personal histories, political ideologies, and leadership styles provides valuable insights into the decision-making processes that shape international relations. By examining their formative experiences, policy priorities, and diplomatic approaches, we can gain a deeper understanding of the motivations behind their actions on the global stage. Through comprehensive analysis, we aim to paint a nuanced picture of these leaders, encompassing their strengths, vulnerabilities, and the complex interplay of domestic and international factors influencing their decision-making. By doing so, we hope to shed light on the intricate web of interpersonal dynamics that underpins modern geopolitics and its potential impact on the evolving Cold War narrative.

Diplomatic Strategies and Missteps

Diplomatic strategies play a crucial role in navigating the complexities of international relations, especially amid political turmoil. In the face of escalating tensions, overt and subtle missteps in diplomatic maneuvering can profoundly affect global stability. Effective strategies require careful consideration of historical context, cultural nuances, and power dynamics. Missteps, on the other hand, can lead to misunderstandings, miscalculations, and even conflict.

One critical aspect of diplomatic strategies is the art of negotiation. Skilled diplomats must balance assertiveness with empathy, understanding the need for compromise without compromising core interests. At the same time, missteps in negotiations can impede progress and perpetuate stalemates, deteriorating relationships between nations. The delicate dance of diplomacy demands careful orchestration to avoid unnecessary escalations and foster constructive dialogue.

Furthermore, the use of public diplomacy and soft power can shape perceptions and build goodwill among nations. Thoughtful communication and cultural exchanges can bridge gaps and promote mutual understanding. However, missteps in public diplomacy, such as inflammatory rhetoric or insensitive gestures, can inflame tensions and erode trust. Diplomatic missteps in this realm can have long-lasting repercussions on the international stage.

Another key consideration is the alignment of diplomatic strategies with economic policies. Trade agreements, sanctions, and financial incentives are often used as tools of diplomacy. Successful economic relations can strengthen alliances and mitigate conflicts. Nevertheless, miscalculations or misuse of economic leverage can backfire, triggering retaliatory measures and exacerbating geopolitical frictions.

Additionally, multilateral engagements through international organizations can provide diplomatic platforms for cooperation and conflict resolution. Effective diplomatic strategies within these forums necessitate adept navigation of diverse agendas and competing interests. Conversely, missteps, including disregard for diplomatic norms or unilateral actions, may undermine collaborative efforts and breed discord.

In conclusion, diplomatic strategies wield significant influence on the global stage, serving as a linchpin for preserving peace and managing crises. By understanding the nuances of effective diplomacy and learning from past missteps, the international community can endeavor to construct a more stable and harmonious world order.

Impact of Domestic Policies on International Relations

Domestic policies profoundly influence international relations, shaping the geopolitical landscape and affecting global dynamics. At the heart of this intricate interplay lies the fundamental principle that a nation's internal decisions have external ramifications. This section delves into the nuanced impact of domestic policies on international relations, exploring how these policies can provoke significant ripple effects across the global stage.

For instance, a nation's economic policies hold immense sway over its international standing. Implementing protectionist trade measures or unilateral tariffs can trigger retaliatory actions from other countries, culminating in trade tensions and potential trade wars. Conversely, fostering an environment conducive to foreign investment and trade liberalization can bolster diplomatic ties and reinforce a country's role in the global economy.

Furthermore, a nation's social and cultural fabric inherently influences its international relationships. Internal socio-cultural policies, such as immigration regulations and human rights initiatives, can reverberate internationally, enhancing or straining diplomatic connections with other nations. For instance, stringent immigration policies may strain bilateral relations, while a commitment to upholding human rights can bolster a country's moral authority and international reputation.

Political ideologies and governance styles also significantly shape a country's international interactions. A government's alignment with autocratic regimes or democratic alliances can engender far-reaching repercussions on diplomatic ties. Additionally, a government's stability or volatility directly impacts its reliability as a diplomatic partner, influencing the level of trust and cooperation it garners from the international community.

In conclusion, the intricacies of domestic policies permeate international relations, exerting a multifaceted impact on the global landscape. By recognizing the interconnected nature of domestic and international affairs, policymakers can navigate the complexities of diplomacy with astuteness and foresight, laying the foundation for robust and sustainable international relationships.

Alliances and Alignments: Shifting Sands

The landscape of international alliances and alignments is constantly changing, shaped by the evolving geopolitical dynamics of the 21st century. As global powers jockey for strategic advantage and seek to safeguard their interests, the traditional patterns of alliance systems have become increasingly malleable. The era following the end of the Cold War witnessed a reconfiguration of alliances with the disintegration of established blocs and the emergence of new regional and functional partnerships. In this context, it is essential to analyze the fluid nature of alliances and how they impact the current geopolitical environment. Nations are constantly reassessing their alliances and recalibrating their foreign policy strategies in response to shifting global power dynamics. The rise of non-state actors, transnational threats, and economic interdependence has added complexity to the alliance-building and maintenance calculus. Hence, the traditional binary framework of alliances has given way to a more intricate web of overlapping and intersecting partnerships. Alliances in the contemporary geopolitical landscape transcend military pacts and encompass various shared interests, from economic cooperation to cultural exchanges. Additionally, the formation of ad hoc coalitions to address specific challenges further underscores the dynamic nature of modern alliances. The intricacies of alignment politics require a nuanced understanding of the interplay between national interests, historical rivalries, and the quest for security and stability. Moreover, technological advancements, such as cyber capabilities and space-based assets, have reshaped the considerations underpinning alliance formations. These changes challenge the traditional assumptions about the durability and predictability of alliances, necessitating a reevaluation of existing frameworks. The ebb and flow of alliances amid geopolitical uncertainties underscores the imperative of flexible and agile foreign policy approaches that can adapt to emergent challenges. As the global order continues to evolve, the intricacies of alliances and alignments will remain pivotal in shaping the contours of international relations, making it essential for policymakers and analysts to comprehend the ever-shifting sands upon which these alliances are built.

Negotiation Tactics under Pressure

In international diplomacy, negotiation tactics come to the forefront amidst delicate and high-stakes scenarios. When under pressure, diplomats and leaders must navigate a complex web of interests, objectives, and potential outcomes. Negotiating under pressure requires a combination of strategic foresight, emotional intelligence, and a nuanced understanding of the counterpart's motivations.

One key aspect of negotiation under pressure is the ability to maintain composure and clarity of thought amidst challenging circumstances. Leaders must demonstrate resilience, poise, and an unwavering commitment to their nation's priorities. Maintaining open lines of communication, even during tense moments, is essential for building trust and fostering constructive dialogue.

Furthermore, negotiation tactics under pressure necessitate a deep understanding of cultural nuances and diplomatic protocols. Recognizing the sensitivities and red lines of the counterpart's position can facilitate more productive negotiations and prevent unintended escalation. Additionally, skilled negotiators must possess the ability to adapt their strategies in real time, responding adeptly to shifting dynamics and unexpected developments.

In high-pressure negotiations, the strategic use of leverage and persuasive communication becomes paramount. Diplomats often engage in a delicate dance of compromise and concession while safeguarding their core interests. The skillful application of hard and soft power can influence the trajectory of negotiations and shape the final agreement.

Moreover, third-party mediation and facilitation cannot be overlooked in negotiations under pressure. Trusted mediators and neutral entities can act as catalysts for progress, offering creative solutions and mitigating tensions between conflicting parties. Utilizing the expertise of professional mediators can inject fresh perspectives and innovative approaches into seemingly intractable negotiations.

An integral aspect of negotiation tactics under pressure is managing public perceptions and domestic expectations.

Leaders must strike a delicate balance between projecting strength and resolve to their constituents while signaling openness to dialogue and cooperation on the global stage. Crafting a cohesive narrative that aligns domestic and international messaging is crucial for sustaining public support amidst challenging negotiations.

In conclusion, negotiation tactics under pressure demand a multifaceted approach that integrates strategic acumen, effective communication, cultural awareness, and adaptability. Successful negotiations in high-stakes scenarios hinge upon the ability to navigate complexities with nuance and finesse, ultimately aiming to achieve mutually beneficial outcomes amidst formidable challenges.

Elections and Leader Legitimacy

In the complex landscape of contemporary geopolitics, understanding the implications of elections on leader legitimacy is crucial. Elections serve as a fundamental mechanism through which leaders gain and maintain power, shaping the dynamics of international relations. This section delves into the multifaceted nature of elections, examining their impact on domestic and global leader legitimacy.

Elections are pivotal moments that reflect the will of the

people and their confidence in the ruling leadership. A leader's legitimacy often hinges on the transparency, fairness, and integrity of the electoral process. Scrutinizing the conduct of elections provides insight into a nation's level of democratic governance and political stability. It also influences how the global community perceives a leader's legitimacy in its international dealings.

The outcome of elections can have profound ramifications for international diplomacy and geopolitical alliances. A change in leadership resulting from elections may lead to shifts in foreign policy, altering a nation's strategic stance. Additionally, a leader's legitimacy post-election can impact other nations' willingness to engage in diplomatic relations, negotiations, or collaborations.

Examining leader legitimacy post-election requires an analysis of the domestic, regional, and global factors at play. Domestic policies and governance directly affect a leader's legitimacy, while regional and global perceptions shape the leader's standing on the world stage. Conversely, the international community's response to the electoral process and its outcomes can influence a leader's legitimacy within their own country.

It is imperative to consider the mechanisms leaders employ to ensure their legitimacy in the face of electoral challenges. This may encompass engaging in meaningful dialogue with opposition parties, upholding democratic values, and working towards national unity. Conversely, actions such as rigging elections, suppressing dissent, or using coercive tactics erode leader legitimacy both domestically and abroad.

Furthermore, the role of international organizations in monitoring and evaluating elections cannot be overstated. Organizations such as the United Nations, the Organization for Security and Co-operation in Europe (OSCE), and regional bodies play a pivotal role in assessing the fairness and transparency of elections. Their observations and recommendations contribute to shaping global perceptions of leader legitimacy and the democratic processes of nations, thereby influencing international partnerships and cooperation.

In conclusion, elections and the ensuing legitimacy of leaders have far-reaching implications for the intricate web of international relations. Understanding the nuances of leader legitimacy in elections is indispensable for comprehending the evolving landscape of global politics.

International Organizations and Their Roles

In the complex arena of international politics, the roles played by international organizations are pivotal in shaping diplomatic outcomes and global stability. These organizations, including the United Nations, the European Union, the North Atlantic Treaty Organization (NATO), and others, serve as platforms for multilateral dialogue, cooperation, and conflict resolution.

The United Nations, established in the aftermath of World War II, remains a cornerstone of international diplomacy. Its various agencies and specialized bodies are entrusted with responsibilities ranging from peacekeeping to humanitarian aid. The Security Council, with its five permanent members and ten rotating members, holds significant sway over matters of peace and security, often serving as a forum for addressing major geopolitical crises.

Similarly, the European Union, rooted in economic collaboration, has evolved into a key political player on the global stage. Its influence extends beyond trade and commerce as it navigates issues related to migration, security, and environmental policy. Though at times fraught with internal tensions, the EU's collective approach to foreign affairs allows for a unified stance in international negotiations.

NATO, a military alliance formed to safeguard the security of its member states, stands as a central pillar of transatlantic cooperation. With its commitment to collective defense, NATO not only serves as a deterrent to aggression but also fosters interoperability among its diverse members. Additionally, it actively manages crises and promotes stability in regions beyond its immediate purview.

Beyond these prominent examples, a myriad of other international bodies, such as the World Trade Organization, the International Monetary Fund, and the World Health Organization, contribute to the global order through their respective areas of expertise. While each organization may face criticisms and limitations, their collective impact underscores the value of multilateral engagement in addressing shared challenges.

Critical to the effectiveness of these organizations is the capacity to adapt to evolving geopolitical dynamics and emerging threats. As non-state actors increasingly shape international affairs, international organizations must remain agile and responsive. Moreover, ensuring equitable representation and decision-making processes within these bodies is essential for fostering trust and legitimacy.

Understanding the roles and functions of international organizations is indispensable for navigating the intricate web of global diplomacy. Whether mediating disputes, coordinating humanitarian efforts, or setting international standards, these entities embody the aspirations of a connected world striving for peace, stability, and prosperity.

Case Studies of Diplomatic Incidents

In this section, we delve into comprehensive case studies that exemplify the intricate nature of diplomatic incidents within the context of the ongoing geopolitical turmoil. The first case study examines the 2014 annexation of Crimea by Russia, a move that sparked international condemnation and a series of diplomatic repercussions. We analyze the intricacies of diplomatic negotiations, the role of international organizations, and the broader implications for regional stability. The second case study delves into the protracted conflict in Syria and the various diplomatic attempts to broker a peaceful resolution. This multifaceted crisis has tested the efficacy of diplomatic intervention, with key players showcasing competing interests and strategies. Moving on, we explore the South China Sea dispute, offering an in-depth analysis of the diplomatic maneuvers and territorial claims that have fueled tensions among neighboring countries and global powers. Additionally, we examine the recent trade disputes between the United States and China, scrutinizing the interplay of economic and diplomatic strategies as both nations navigate complex bilateral relations. These case studies provide valuable insight into the intricate web of diplomatic incidents, offering profound lessons for understanding the challenges and opportunities inherent in contemporary international relations.

Conclusion: The Way Forward in Diplomacy

As we conclude this exploration of diplomacy in the context of evolving geopolitical dynamics, it becomes evident that the way forward in diplomacy demands a multifaceted approach that addresses the complexity and interconnectedness of contemporary global relations. Building upon the lessons learned from the case studies of diplomatic incidents discussed earlier, policymakers, diplomats, and leaders need to prioritize cultivating robust, transparent, and inclusive channels of communication and negotiation. This necessitates a departure from unilateralism and a reaffirmation of the value of multilateral diplomacy underpinned by respect for international law and norms.

Furthermore, the future of diplomacy hinges on adapting to emerging challenges while upholding fundamental principles of human rights, democratic governance, and sustainable development. The evolving nature of technology presents both opportunities and threats in the realm of diplomacy, thus requiring careful consideration of cybersecurity, digital sovereignty, and ethical standards in the conduct of statecraft. Nations must invest in building strategic cyber capabilities, fostering resilience against disinformation campaigns, and leveraging technology as a force for constructive international engagement.

A pivotal aspect of the way forward in diplomacy lies in recalibrating diplomatic strategies to address non-traditional security issues, such as climate change, pandemics, and transnational crime. Recognizing that these challenges transcend borders and affect global stability, effective diplomacy must integrate efforts to mitigate environmental risks, promote public health cooperation, and combat illicit networks. Embracing an approach of preventive diplomacy and conflict resolution, as well as championing humanitarian diplomacy, will be central to advancing sustainable peace and prosperity.

Finally, the way forward in diplomacy necessitates a recommitment to fostering intercultural dialogue, understanding, and cooperation. Promoting mutual respect, tolerance, and cross-cultural exchange is indispensable in shaping a more harmonious and interconnected world in an era marked by ideological divisions and cultural tensions. This includes amplifying the role of cultural diplomacy, people-to-people exchanges, and educational partnerships to build bridges across societies and advance shared aspirations for a peaceful and collaborative global order.

By embracing these guiding principles and recognizing the imperative of proactive and principled diplomacy, the international community can navigate the intricacies of the contemporary geopolitical landscape with wisdom, foresight, and a steadfast commitment to the common good.

Chapter Eight

Media Battles: Propaganda and Public Perception

Modern Media Warfare

Media has emerged as a potent weapon in warfare and political maneuvering in the contemporary geopolitical landscape. The convergence of traditional mass media, social networking platforms, and information technology has revolutionized the dissemination of news, propaganda, and disinformation, effectively reshaping the battlefield of public opinion. Media utilization as a strategic tool for shaping narratives, influencing perceptions, and swaying public sentiment has become a defining aspect of modern conflict. This paradigm shift warrants a comprehensive examination of the multifaceted dimensions of modern media warfare. The ability to manipulate public discourse, manage international image, and conceal military intentions through the orchestration of media content has magnified the strategic significance of media in global affairs. Consequently, understanding modern media warfare's evolution, dynamics, and implications is indispensable for comprehending contemporary international relations. To navigate these complexities, it is essential to analyze historical precedents, technological advancements, psychological underpinnings, and ethical considerations surrounding media warfare. This section will delve into the transformative impact of media on geopolitical strategies, the deployment of information as a weapon, and the intricate interplay between traditional journalism and state-sponsored propaganda. Moreover, it will scrutinize how governments, insurgent groups, and non-state actors exploit the informational ecosystem to wage conflicts that transcend physical battlefields. By delineating the entwined nature of politics, communication, and armed conflict within the context of modern media warfare, this exploration aims to uncover the nuanced mechanisms driving contemporary international power plays.

Historical Overview of Propaganda in International Conflicts

The history of propaganda in international conflicts is a complex tapestry woven into the fabric of human civilization. From the ancient use of symbols and oral storytelling to the modern era of digital communication, nations, and entities have strategically utilized propaganda to sway public opinion, demonize adversaries, and rally support for their cause. The earliest recorded instances of propaganda can be traced back to ancient civilizations, where rulers and political leaders employed art, rhetoric, and religious symbolism to promote their agendas and legitimize their authority. As societies evolved, so did the methods of propaganda. In times of conflict, such as during the World Wars, governments and military organizations sharpened their use of propaganda to manipulate information and shape national narratives. The emergence of mass media in the 20th century propelled propaganda onto a global stage, enabling states to broadcast their messages across borders and influence international opinion. Notable examples include the Soviet Union's dissemination of communist ideology during the Cold War and Nazi Germany's infamous propaganda machine under the leadership of Joseph Goebbels. The coalescence of propaganda with technological advancements has further transformed its efficacy. The contemporary landscape of propaganda in international conflicts encompasses sophisticated tactics, including psychological operations, false flag operations, and targeted disinformation campaigns. The integration of social media platforms into the domain of propaganda has facilitated the rapid dissemination of narratives and amplified the impact of misinformation. It is imperative to recognize that propaganda is not solely a tool of authoritarian regimes but is also present in democratic societies, albeit with different manifestations. The study of historical propaganda in international conflicts provides invaluable insights into the enduring strategies and evolving methodologies used to shape public perception and manipulate information in pursuit of geopolitical goals.

The Role of State-Controlled Media

State-controlled media has historically played a significant role in shaping public opinion and influencing perceptions both domestically and internationally. In the context of the new cold war, state-backed media outlets have become powerful tools for advancing strategic narratives, disseminating propaganda, and exerting influence on a global scale. These media entities are often closely aligned with the government's political agenda and serve as mouthpieces for official viewpoints, thereby amplifying a particular ideological perspective. Through extensive resources and centralized control, state-controlled media organizations possess the capacity to shape narratives, drive agendas, and construct portrayals of events that align with national interests. Additionally, they can be leveraged to discredit adversaries, distort information, and create a distorted reality. In some cases, such media outlets operate with limited editorial independence, resulting in biased reporting and the exclusion of dissenting voices. The impact of state-controlled media extends beyond domestic audiences, as these platforms are utilized to project influence on an international scale. By shaping narratives and controlling information flows, these entities seek to mold global perceptions, generate support for strategic initiatives, and foster alliances while undermining perceived opponents. They serve as instruments of soft power, projecting a favorable image of the state while disparaging rival nations. Furthermore, the use of state-controlled media is intertwined with diplomatic efforts, serving as a means to extend influence, shape opinion, and advance foreign policy objectives. As the battle for influence intensifies in the digital age, state-controlled media also leverages technological advancements, targeting audiences through online platforms and social media channels. This enables the dissemination of tailored content to specific demographics, amplifying reach and impact. However, it also raises concerns about the spread of disinformation and manipulation, highlighting the need for increased vigilance and critical evaluation. Recognizing the prevalence and influence of state-controlled media, it is imperative to analyze its role within the broader landscape of information warfare and consider strategies to counter its potential negative implications.

Independent Media and Alternative Perspec-

tives

In the age of information warfare, independent media outlets and alternative perspectives play a crucial role in shaping public discourse and countering state-controlled narratives. Independent media organizations strive to provide diverse viewpoints, investigative journalism, and critical analyses that challenge official accounts and offer a more comprehensive understanding of complex international conflicts. These outlets often serve as watchdogs, uncovering truths that government-controlled sources might suppress or misrepresent. By promoting transparency and accountability, independent media help to ensure that the public has access to a wide range of information and opinions. Moreover, they offer a platform for dissenting voices and marginalized communities whose stories may be overlooked or distorted by mainstream channels. In situations of geopolitical tension and propaganda-driven narratives, independent media can serve as a beacon of truth, offering nuanced perspectives that contribute to fostering informed and critical citizenship. Additionally, the digital age has expanded the reach of independent media, allowing for the dissemination of uncensored information across borders, thereby shaping global opinion and challenging hegemonic narratives. However, independent media also face significant challenges, including financial constraints, political pressure, and even physical threats to journalists and their sources. As such, defending and supporting independent media is essential for maintaining a diverse and vibrant information ecosystem that empowers the public to engage with complex geopolitical issues critically. Ultimately, the vitality and resilience of independent media and alternative perspectives are fundamental for safeguarding democratic principles and upholding the right to access pluralistic and unfiltered information.

Social Media: Amplifying Disinformation and Dissent

Social media has become an amplified platform for the dissemination of disinformation and the propagation of dissent in the context of modern conflicts. With its pervasive reach and instantaneous nature, social media platforms have presented both opportunities and challenges in shaping public opinion and influencing perceptions during geopolitical tensions. The unrestricted flow of information and opinion on these platforms has created an environment ripe for the spread of falsehoods, leading to heightened polarization and erosion of trust within societies. It is paramount to understand the dynamics through which social media amplifies disinformation and dissent, as well as the implications it carries for international relations. While social media offers a democratized space for diverse voices and alternative narratives, it also enables the rapid proliferation of misinformation and propaganda, often without accountability or verifiable sources. This unrestricted environment provides hostile actors with unprecedented opportunities to manipulate narratives, influence public sentiment, and escalate conflicts. Moreover, the viral nature of content on social media can rapidly amplify dissenting views, exacerbating societal divisions and destabilizing diplomatic efforts. The unchecked dissemination of disinformation through social media has the potential to inflame existing tensions, sow discord among populations, and undermine diplomatic initiatives aimed at conflict resolution. Recognizing the predominant role that social media plays in shaping public discourse, governments, international organizations, and civil society must prioritize efforts to counter disinformation and instill critical media literacy skills among citizens. Initiatives focusing on promoting digital media literacy, fact-checking, and responsible online behavior are pivotal in fostering resilience against the manipulation of information and narratives. Effective regulation and oversight of social media platforms, while upholding principles of free expression, are essential to curtail the spread of harmful disinformation and mitigate its deleterious impact on public perception during times of conflict. By addressing the challenges posed by social media in amplifying disinformation and dissent, stakeholders can work toward fostering an informed and discerning global audience, bolstering the prospects for constructive dialogue and peaceful resolution of geopolitical crises.

Information Warfare Tactics and Techniques

Information warfare has become an integral component of modern conflict, employing a diverse array of tactics and techniques to shape narratives, manipulate perceptions, and influence decision-making. This chapter delves into the multifaceted strategies employed in contemporary information warfare, shedding light on the intricate web of tactics and techniques. At its core, information warfare seeks to exploit the vulnerabilities of communication channels and exploit the psychological susceptibility of target audiences. Redefining traditional notions of combat, the battlefield of information warfare transcends physical borders and engages in a battle for hearts and minds. One of the quintessential tactics within information warfare is the dissemination of disinformation and false narratives through various media platforms. This encompasses the deliberate spread of misleading, inaccurate, or fabricated content with the intent to sow discord, undermine trust, and manipulate public opinion. Concurrently, the manipulation of social media algorithms and utilization of coordinated bot networks present potent tools for amplifying certain narratives while suppressing opposing viewpoints. The orchestration of coordinated smear campaigns, astroturfing, and false flags are additional insidious tactics leveraged to discredit adversaries and sow confusion among target populations. Furthermore, the infiltration of cyber domains and digital infrastructure serves as a pivotal avenue for conducting disruptive operations, ranging from strategic data breaches to orchestrated cyber-attacks. These initiatives aim to destabilize critical infrastructure, paralyze communication networks, and subvert organizational functionalities. Psychological operations form another critical facet of information warfare, employing targeted messaging and tailored narratives to exploit cognitive biases, nurture uncertainty, and foment societal unrest. Leveraging advancements in big data analytics, adversarial entities meticulously profile and segment target audiences, enabling the personalized delivery of carefully curated propaganda that resonates with individual susceptibilities. Preying on emotional triggers and cultural fault lines, these operations seek to radicalize and polarize communities, portraying adversaries in a negative light while exalting their own narratives. The weaponization of deepfakes, AI-generated content, and synthetic media adds an unprecedented dimension to information warfare, blurring the line between reality and fiction. This enables adversaries to fabricate compelling audio-visual content, forging falsified instances and speeches to incite turmoil or discredit individuals and institutions. Moreover, the cultivation of front organizations and sympathetic influencers facilitates the clandestine propagation of specific agendas, further perpetuating a distorted information landscape. In steering through these treacherous waters, countering information warfare necessitates a vigorous, multi-faceted approach encompassing media literacy initiatives, robust fact-checking frameworks, enhanced cybersecurity measures, and concerted international collaborations to uphold the integrity of information ecosystems.

Psychological Impact on Public Opinion

Understanding the psychological impact on public opinion is imperative in the realm of media battles and information warfare. The pervasive influence of media messaging, whether through traditional outlets or social media platforms, profoundly shapes the perceptions and attitudes of the populace. Psychological research has demonstrated the persuasive power of well-crafted narratives, emotional appeals, and visual imagery in swaying public opinion. Beyond mere dissemination of information, media content often carries embedded cues that trigger the audience's cognitive biases, emotional responses, and behavioral inclinations.

The phenomenon of confirmation bias, wherein individuals gravitate towards information that aligns with their existing beliefs and values, plays a significant role in reinforcing preconceived notions and ideological stances. Media entities, cognizant of this human tendency, strategically tailor their narratives to resonate with specific audience segments, thereby solidifying support or dissent for particular causes or actors. Furthermore, the emotive framing of stories and events can evoke empathy, outrage, or fear, eliciting corresponding reactions from the public and influencing their subsequent behavior and decision-making.

Cognitive dissonance, another psychological construct, comes into play when individuals encounter conflicting information that challenges their established worldview. Media campaigns leveraging this phenomenon seek to engender doubt or skepticism in opposing viewpoints, potentially destabilizing confidence in alternative perspectives. Additionally, the use of social proof, wherein individuals look to the actions and opinions of others as a guide for their own behavior, underscores the importance of cultivating and controlling public narratives to sway opinion en masse.

Moreover, the psychological impact extends beyond immediate belief formation to societal dynamics and intergroup relations. Media representations and framing can shape perceptions of 'in-groups' and 'out-groups', contributing to polarization, prejudice, and social division. As such, the ramifications of media battles extend far beyond the dissemination of information, exerting a deep-seated influence on individual mentalities and collective identity.

Understanding the psychological underpinnings of media influence on public opinion is crucial for deciphering the complexities of contemporary information warfare and devising strategies to promote informed critical thinking and civic resilience amidst the relentless tidal wave of persuasive messaging.

Case Studies of Successful Media Influences

During the course of modern history, numerous conflicts have been shaped by the profound impact of media influences on public perception and international opinion. This section will analyze specific instances where media played a decisive role in shaping the outcomes of geopolitical struggles. One such case study is the role of media in the Gulf War of 1990-1991, where extensive media coverage provided real-time updates of the conflict, resulting in heightened public awareness and engagement. The images of precision-guided bombings and news reports depicting the suffering of civilians captured the attention of global audiences, influencing political decisions and perceptions of the war. Another compelling case is the Rwandan genocide in 1994, where local radio stations were used to propagate hate speech and incite violence, leading to mass atrocities. The unchecked dissemination of vitriolic messages through the media had a devastating impact on societal stability and humanitarian efforts in the region. Furthermore, the ongoing conflict in Syria has demonstrated how competing narratives and visual representations in the media can shape international responses and interventions. Various stakeholders have strategically utilized media platforms to garner support, portray their adversaries negatively, and rally international assistance. These case studies underscore the critical role of media in conflict dynamics, underscoring the need for a comprehensive understanding of its power and ethical responsibilities. They also highlight the enduring relevance of media literacy and the need for regulatory oversight to ensure that informational integrity prevails in times of crisis.

Regulatory and Ethical Considerations in Media Operations

In the context of modern geopolitical conflicts, media operations play a crucial role in shaping public perception and opinion. As such, regulatory and ethical considerations are paramount to ensure the integrity and credibility of media content. This section delves into the complex landscape of media regulations and the ethical dilemmas that often arise in the midst of information warfare. Regulatory frameworks differ across countries and regions, with varying levels of government oversight and control. Balancing the need for freedom of expression with the responsibility to prevent misinformation and propaganda presents a significant challenge. Ethical considerations in media operations encompass issues such as truthfulness, objectivity, and the potential impact of media content on societal harmony. The evolving nature of digital media and the proliferation of online platforms have further complicated regulatory and ethical standards. As technology continues to advance, questions arise about the accountability of tech companies in monitoring and regulating content. Furthermore, the global nature of information dissemination necessitates international cooperation in setting ethical norms and regulatory guidelines. This section explores the efforts of international organizations and alliances to establish common principles for media operations in the context of conflict. The delicate balance between upholding freedom of speech and preventing the spread of harmful propaganda requires a nuanced approach that respects diverse cultural and political contexts. Ultimately, effective regulatory and ethical considerations in media operations are essential for maintaining the integrity of information in the face of the relentless media battles characteristic of modern geopolitical conflicts.

Countering Misinformation: Strategies and Efforts

Countering misinformation has become a paramount concern for governments, organizations, and individuals alike in an age characterized by the rapid dissemination of information through various media platforms. Multifaceted strategies and concerted efforts are essential to combat the virulent spread of false narratives and propaganda. This section delves into the nuanced approaches and initiatives aimed at addressing the pervasive challenge of misinformation.

One pivotal strategy in countering misinformation is the promotion of media literacy and critical thinking skills. Empowering individuals to discern and evaluate information critically makes them less susceptible to falling prey to deceptive content. Education campaigns that emphasize digital literacy and fact-checking have proven to be effective in enhancing public resilience against misinformation.

Collaborative partnerships between tech companies, government entities, and civil society organizations have also yielded significant advancements in thwarting the proliferation of misleading information. By implementing fact-checking tools, algorithmic adjustments, and content moderation practices, these alliances strive to stem the dissemination of false and harmful content across online platforms.

Furthermore, the cultivation of transparent and accountable media practices serves as a linchpin in the battle against misinformation. Journalistic integrity, adherence to ethical reporting standards, and the amplification of diverse voices are pivotal in fortifying the veracity of information disseminated to the public. Initiatives that bolster media pluralism and support independent investigative journalism contribute to the cultivation of a robust, truth-driven media landscape.

An integral component of countering misinformation involves proactively debunking falsehoods and conspiracy theories. Rapid response teams and dedicated debunking platforms are crucial in swiftly dispelling emerging misinformation before it gains traction. Equipping fact-checkers with the necessary resources and infrastructure bolsters their capacity to refute spurious claims effectively.

Additionally, leveraging technological advancements such as artificial intelligence and data analytics can enhance the detection and mitigation of misinformation. Machine learning algorithms have the potential to identify patterns of disinformation and flag dubious content, enabling swift intervention and corrective measures.

Amidst the efforts to counter misinformation, emphasis must also be placed on fostering a culture of transparency and accountability within the media ecosystem. Establishing clear channels for feedback, corrections, and retractions fosters public trust and confidence in media institutions.

Ultimately, countering misinformation demands sustained vigilance, collaborative interventions, and unwavering commitment to upholding the sanctity of truth. By synergizing educational, technological, and ethical imperatives, societies can proactively confront misinformation and safeguard the integrity of public discourse.

Chapter Nine

Future Forecasts: Scenarios for Peace and Conflict

Global Forecasting

The study of global politics requires a comprehensive understanding of the ever-evolving geopolitical landscape and the complex interplay of international actors, making it imperative to employ forecasting methodologies that can offer valuable insights into potential future scenarios. Global forecasting involves analyzing current geopolitical trends, economic indicators, military technologies, and diplomatic strategies to anticipate the possible trajectories of international relations and conflicts. This section aims to delve into the various forecasting models used in global politics and introduce the methodological approach for predicting future scenarios in this dynamic arena.

At its core, global forecasting seeks to anticipate potential outcomes based on an analysis of existing factors, including political, economic, social, technological, environmental, and military aspects. By employing robust analytical tools and methodologies, such as scenario planning, trend analysis, and risk assessment, forecasters can gain a more profound understanding of the driving forces shaping global politics and identify potential challenges and opportunities that lie ahead.

Analyzing Current Geopolitical Trends

As we navigate the complex tapestry of global relations, it is imperative to analyze the prevailing geopolitical trends shaping our world meticulously. The evolving nature of power dynamics among nations is at the forefront of this analysis. The emergence of new economic powers, such as China and India, alongside traditional giants like the United States and Russia, has led to a reconfiguration of global influence, challenging established norms and alliances. Additionally, regional tensions and conflicts continue to impact international stability, from the South China Sea disputes to the ongoing conflicts in the Middle East, illustrating the interconnectedness of geopolitics. Furthermore, the increasing prominence of non-state actors, including transnational corporations and influential interest groups, adds layers of complexity to the geopolitical landscape. These entities wield significant power and influence, often transcending national boundaries, thereby necessitating a recalibration of traditional analytical frameworks. The rising significance of technological advancements, particularly in the realms of cyber warfare and artificial intelligence, further complicates geopolitical dynamics, creating new avenues for competition and conflict. Moreover, environmental pressures, such as climate change and resource scarcity, are becoming key determinants in geopolitical decision-making as countries vie for strategic advantages amidst shifting ecological paradigms. In parallel, the role of international institutions, including the United Nations and regional organizations, continues to evolve, shaping how states interact and cooperate on the global stage. The interplay between these multifaceted factors underscores the intricate mosaic that defines current geopolitical trends, requiring nuanced scrutiny and prescient foresight to anticipate and navigate the complexities that lie ahead.

Economic Indicators and Their Implications

In the contemporary landscape of global affairs, economic indicators serve as essential barometers for predicting and understanding the potential trajectories of international relations and geopolitical stability. This section delves into the intricate web of economic variables and their far-reaching implications in the context of evolving Cold War dynamics.

As nations jostle for supremacy in an increasingly interconnected world, economic indicators play a pivotal role in shaping strategic calculations and foreign policy decisions. Gross Domestic Product (GDP), trade balances, inflation rates, and employment figures are among the key metrics scrutinized by policymakers and analysts to gauge a country's economic health. The interplay of these indicators not only reflects a nation's internal economic strength but also influences its external relationships and power dynamics on the global stage.

Furthermore, the interconnectedness of today's economies amplifies the reverberations of economic shifts across borders. A downturn in one major economy can trigger a domino effect, impacting markets and industries worldwide. Understanding these complex interdependencies and their potential cascading effects is crucial for anticipating the spillover of economic crises into the realm of international politics and security.

Moreover, the weaponization of economic tools, such as sanctions and tariffs, has emerged as a prominent feature of modern statecraft. By leveraging economic leverage points, states seek to advance their strategic agendas, coerce adversaries, or safeguard their national interests. This confluence of economics and geopolitics underscores the need for a comprehensive understanding of economic indicators and their multifaceted implications within the broader context of global power play.

Economic indicators offer insights into nations' prosperity and stability and serve as precursors to potential geopolitical flashpoints. Shifting trade patterns, currency fluctuations, and resource scarcity can all sow the seeds of diplomatic friction and conflict. The intertwined nature of economics and geopolitics necessitates a nuanced approach to forecasting and strategizing peace and security in an era defined by economic interdependence and competition.

In summary, examining economic indicators and their implications unveils the intricate interconnections between economic dynamics and international relations. As we navigate the complexities of the new Cold War, a deep comprehension of these interactions becomes indispensable for envisioning scenarios for both peace and conflict and formulating effective policies and strategies that resonate with the realities of a rapidly evolving global landscape.

Military Technologies and Future Warfare

As the global geopolitical landscape continues to evolve, the role of military technologies in shaping future warfare scenarios cannot be understated. Rapid technological advancements have led to unprecedented capabilities and complexities in defense and security. Artificial intelligence, unmanned aerial vehicles (UAVs), autonomous weapons systems, and cyber warfare are just a few examples of the cutting-edge technologies redefining modern warfare. These developments bring both opportunities and challenges as nations strive to stay ahead in the arms race while adhering to international norms and ethical considerations. Integrating AI into military applications can revolutionize command and control, logistics, intelligence gathering, and even decision-making processes on the battlefield. However, concerns regarding the ethical use of AI in warfare, autonomous weapons, and the potential for unintended consequences loom large. Furthermore, the proliferation of asymmetrical warfare, where non-state actors and rogue elements harness disruptive technologies to undermine conventional forces, poses a significant threat to global stability. Therefore, it becomes imperative for policymakers and military strategists to grapple with the implications of these technological advancements and their impact on future conflict scenarios. Additionally, the interplay between space-based capabilities, electromagnetic spectrum dominance, and the militarization of cyberspace presents a multifaceted arena for potential confrontations. The strategic implications of these domains in modern warfare underscore the need for comprehensive defense strategies that encompass traditional land, sea, and air capabilities and extend to space and cyberspace. Moreover, the prospect of hybrid warfare – blending conventional and unconventional tactics, including information operations and psychological warfare – further complicates the strategic calculus. Consequently, nations must continually adapt their military doctrines, invest in research and development, and collaborate with allies to effectively address the challenges posed by these emergent technologies. In essence, the evolving landscape of military technologies and their impact on future warfare demands a proactive approach to understanding, regulating, and leveraging these advancements in the service of international peace and security.

Diplomatic Strategies for Conflict Resolution

Diplomatic strategies play a crucial role in resolving conflicts on the international stage. In the new Cold War context, where tensions are high and potential confrontations loom large, effective diplomatic engagement is essential to prevent escalation and foster peaceful resolutions. Diplomatic efforts encompass a range of tactics and approaches, each tailored to the specific circumstances of a given conflict.

One of the primary diplomatic strategies involves mediation, where a neutral third party facilitates communication and negotiation between conflicting parties. Skilled mediators work to identify common ground, build trust, and guide discussions toward mutually acceptable solutions. Additionally, diplomacy relies on diplomatic channels and backchannel communications, allowing for discreet dialogue and negotiation away from the public eye.

Another key aspect of the diplomatic strategy is the employment of multilateral negotiations and forums. International organizations such as the United Nations, the European Union, and regional bodies provide platforms for dialogue and collaboration among nations. These venues offer opportunities for consensus-building, coalition-forming, and establishing shared norms and standards, all of which are fundamental in defusing tensions and building frameworks for cooperation.

Furthermore, diplomatic strategies often emphasize pursuing confidence-building measures (CBMs) to mitigate mistrust and enhance transparency between adversaries. CBMs can take various forms, including arms control agreements, military-to-military dialogues, and joint crisis management exercises. By promoting transparency and predictability, CBMs reduce the risk of miscalculation and inadvertent conflict.

Moreover, the practice of preventive diplomacy encompasses various proactive measures to address emerging sources of tension before they escalate into full-blown crises. This can involve early warning systems, fact-finding missions, and sustained stakeholder engagement to address underlying grievances and fears. Preventive diplomacy requires astute analysis, persistent dialogue, and a willingness to intervene diplomatically at critical junctures.

Lastly, the use of public diplomacy and Track II diplomacy can be instrumental in shaping public opinion, facilitating people-to-people exchanges, and fostering understanding across borders. These efforts help cultivate an environment conducive to peaceful coexistence and collaborative problem-solving.

In conclusion, diplomatic strategies for conflict resolution necessitate nuanced approaches, adept negotiators, and strategic leveraging of international institutions and norms. In the new Cold War context, effective diplomacy stands as a linchpin in steering global relations away from conflict towards sustainable peace and cooperation.

The Role of International Organizations

International organizations play a crucial role in managing and mitigating global conflicts. These organizations serve as platforms for multilateral dialogue and cooperation, providing avenues for diplomacy and negotiation to address complex geopolitical challenges. The United Nations (UN), the European Union (EU), the North Atlantic Treaty Organization (NATO), and various regional organizations all contribute to peace and security efforts worldwide. International organizations facilitate conflict resolution through their structures and mechanisms by promoting dialogue, mediating disputes, and fostering reconciliation between conflicting parties.

One of the key functions of international organizations is to provide a neutral ground for diplomatic engagement. By offering a forum for dialogue, these entities enable nations to engage in peaceful negotiations and find common ground on contentious issues. Furthermore, international organizations often leverage their collective influence to encourage adherence to international law and norms, thereby creating a framework for addressing conflicts within a legal and ethical framework.

Moreover, international organizations support peacebuilding and conflict prevention initiatives by providing humanitarian aid, facilitating peacekeeping operations, and promoting sustainable development in post-conflict regions. These efforts aim to address the root causes of conflicts and foster long-term stability. Additionally, international organizations contribute to conflict resolution by monitoring ceasefire agreements, promoting disarmament, and overseeing the implementation of peace treaties.

In the context of the book's focus on the new Cold War, international organizations also play a critical role in managing tensions between major powers and navigating rivalries. Their ability to convene summits, mediate disputes, and uphold international norms can help prevent conflicts from escalating into full-blown confrontations. Furthermore, by fostering dialogue and collaboration among member states, international organizations work towards building trust and fostering cooperative relationships, which are essential in reducing the risk of conflict.

As the world becomes increasingly interconnected, international organizations also address transnational security challenges such as terrorism, cyber threats, and environmental crises. Their collaborative efforts in areas of mutual concern contribute to enhancing global security and stability. By promoting cross-border cooperation and coordination, these organizations strengthen the collective response to emerging security threats and help build resilience against potential sources of conflict.

In conclusion, the role of international organizations in conflict resolution and peacebuilding is multifaceted and significant. Their capacity to facilitate diplomatic dialogue, promote adherence to international norms, and address the root causes of conflicts underscores their instrumental role in maintaining global stability. As the dynamics of geopolitical competition continue to evolve, international organizations remain vital in shaping a more secure and peaceful world.

Public Opinion and Its Impact on Policy

Public opinion plays a crucial role in shaping the policies of governments and international organizations. The attitudes and perceptions of the general populace can significantly influence the decision-making processes of political leaders and policymakers around the world. Understanding how public opinion affects policy is essential for forecasting future trends in global relations and conflicts.

The impact of public opinion on policy formation is evident in various scenarios, ranging from diplomatic negotiations to military interventions. In democratic societies, policymakers are sensitive to the preferences and concerns of their constituents, as they rely on public support for legitimacy and reelection. As a result, public sentiment often determines the priorities of government agendas and the allocation of resources toward domestic and foreign policy initiatives.

Moreover, public opinion's influence extends beyond national borders, affecting the stance of international organizations and alliances. For instance, the public perception of a humanitarian crisis or conflict can pressure governments to engage in diplomatic efforts or provide humanitarian aid. Similarly, public opposition to military interventions can constrain the actions of governments and multilateral institutions.

In the digital age, social media and online platforms have amplified the impact of public opinion on policymaking. Information spreads rapidly, allowing individuals to express their views and mobilize support for specific causes on a global scale. A single viral hashtag or video can galvanize public opinion and prompt leaders to address pressing issues or revise their policies to align with popular sentiment.

However, the relationship between public opinion and policy has complexities and challenges. Public perceptions can be influenced by misinformation, propaganda, and biased media narratives, leading to misconceptions and polarization. In some cases, public opinion may fluctuate based on fleeting emotions or a limited understanding of intricate geopolitical dynamics, posing dilemmas for policymakers seeking long-term, sustainable solutions.

Nevertheless, public engagement and dialogue are essential for fostering informed opinions and constructive feedback that can guide policymakers toward prudent decisions. By promoting transparency and accountability, governments and international organizations can build trust with their citizens and leverage public input to shape more effective and ethical policies.

Analysts and policymakers must monitor public opinion trends and conduct comprehensive surveys to gauge the evolving attitudes of diverse populations. This proactive approach enables policymakers to anticipate potential shifts in public sentiment and consider the societal implications of their policy choices. Moreover, cultivating open communication channels with the public fosters a sense of civic participation and ownership of collective decisions, nurturing a more inclusive and responsive governance framework.

In conclusion, public opinion is a vital force shaping the trajectory of global policy and conflict resolution. Recognizing the significance of public sentiment and actively engaging with diverse perspectives is indispensable for fostering stability, progress, and consensus in the complex landscape of international relations.

Scenario Planning: Peaceful Resolutions

In global geopolitics, scenario planning for peaceful resolutions offers a crucial framework for understanding the potential pathways to de-escalate tensions and work toward sustainable peace. This section analyzes and outlines plausible scenarios that could lead to diplomatic solutions and collaborative efforts to mitigate conflicts across various regions. As we delve into this complex subject, it is important to emphasize the significance of proactive diplomacy, mediated negotiations, and the collective will to prioritize dialogue over discord.

One potential scenario for peaceful resolution involves multilateral diplomatic initiatives to foster trust and confidence-building measures between conflicting parties. This approach may entail the establishment of bilateral or regional forums where stakeholders can engage in sustained dialogue, exchange viewpoints, and seek common ground on contentious issues. In such scenarios, the involvement of neutral mediators or international organizations can play a pivotal role in facilitating constructive discussions and promoting mutual understanding.

Furthermore, another plausible path toward peaceful resolution revolves around economic interdependence and leveraging trade and investment as tools for fostering cooperation. By exploring mutually beneficial economic partnerships and incentives, nations in conflict could find avenues for shared prosperity, diminishing the incentives for belligerent actions and creating a conducive environment for peaceful coexistence. In this scenario, the role of economic and financial experts and policymakers becomes paramount in devising frameworks that encourage economic collaboration and mutual benefit.

Additionally, engaging in cultural and educational exchanges represents a compelling scenario for fostering long-term peaceful resolutions. By promoting cross-cultural understanding and nurturing people-to-people connections, societies can develop empathy and appreciation for diverse perspectives, ultimately laying the foundation for harmonious cohabitation. Educational institutions, civil society organizations, and grassroots movements can serve as conduits for promoting cultural dialogue, tolerance, and respect for diversity, contributing to developing a global citizenry committed to peaceful coexistence.

As we explore these hypothetical scenarios, we must recognize that achieving a peaceful resolution in complex geopolitical conflicts often demands converging multifaceted strategies. Whether through diplomatic brinkmanship, economic enticements, or societal engagement, successful peaceful resolutions require sustained commitment, strategic foresight, and the collective dedication of international actors toward building a more peaceful and secure world.

Scenario Planning: Escalation of Conflict

In assessing the potential for escalation of conflict in the context of the new Cold War, it is essential to consider a range of precarious scenarios that could unfold. One such scenario involves an aggressive military move by one of the major powers, triggering a chain reaction of defensive responses from allies and regional actors. This could result in heightened tensions and a dangerous spiral toward open warfare. It is imperative to closely examine the impact of such actions on global stability and security architecture.

Moreover, the specter of proxy conflicts cannot be overlooked. Various historical precedents show that international power struggles have often materialized through indirect confrontations in third-party countries. In the modern context, this could manifest as intensifying support for opposing factions in volatile regions, exacerbating existing conflicts and creating new fronts for hostilities.

Beyond traditional warfare, cyber conflict presents a distinct dimension of potential escalation. Sophisticated cyberattacks targeting critical infrastructure, communication networks, and financial systems could destabilize societies and provoke retaliatory measures. The evolving landscape of cyber warfare warrants careful consideration when assessing the pathways to escalation.

Additionally, the possibility of economic warfare cannot be discounted. Trade embargoes, currency manipulation, and non-military sanctions can serve as coercive instruments in the arsenal of statecraft. A concerted effort by major powers to exert economic pressure on adversaries could escalate tensions and precipitate widespread repercussions in the global economy.

It is crucial to analyze how diplomatic channels may either mitigate or exacerbate conflict escalation. Disruptions in international negotiations, breakdowns in diplomatic relations, and mutual expulsion of diplomats could signal a dangerous shift towards heightened confrontation. Conversely, sustained dialogue and mediation efforts could provide avenues for de-escalation and crisis management.

In detailing these potential pathways to conflict escalation, it is paramount to underscore the devastating human cost accompanying such trajectories. The displacement of populations, humanitarian crises, and the erosion of fundamental rights represent sobering realities. Moreover, the threat of nuclear proliferation and the harrowing specter of weapons of mass destruction loom ominously in the backdrop of escalating conflicts, underscoring the imperative of preventive action and conflict resolution.

Foremost, the comprehensive evaluation of these scenarios must serve as a clarion call for proactive policy measures aimed at conflict prevention and resolution. The vital importance of fostering multilateral cooperation, strengthening international norms, and nurturing effective conflict mediation mechanisms cannot be overstated. Timely and decisive actions grounded in diplomacy, strategic foresight, and collaborative peacemaking are indispensable in averting the perilous course of conflict escalation.

Conclusion and Policy Recommendations

In conclusion, the complex dynamics and potential scenarios outlined in this analysis underscore the critical need for proactive policy measures to safeguard global peace and security. As we contemplate the sobering prospects of escalating conflict, policymakers, international organizations, and diplomatic entities must prioritize dialogue, cooperation, and strategic interventions. In light of the evolving geopolitical landscape, a comprehensive framework must be established to mitigate the risk of conflict escalation and promote sustainable peace. This necessitates a multi-faceted approach encompassing economic incentives, diplomatic engagement, and leveraging technological advancements for peaceful resolutions.

Policy recommendations tailored to these pressing concerns include fostering robust diplomatic channels for open communication and negotiation among conflicting parties. Moreover, addressing underlying socioeconomic disparities and inequities can serve as a foundation for long-term stability and peaceful coexistence. Furthermore, the merit of collaborative efforts through international forums cannot be overstated, emphasizing the shared responsibility of the global community in averting catastrophic conflict escalations.

Additionally, policymakers must harness the power of innovative technologies in conflict prevention and resolution. From utilizing advanced analytics for early warning systems to promoting cyber diplomacy, there exists a spectrum of untapped potential for technology-driven peacebuilding initiatives. Embracing these solutions aligns with the imperative to anticipate and counteract the drivers of conflict, thereby fostering resilient structures that uphold global stability.

Furthermore, strengthening existing frameworks for arms control and disarmament will play a pivotal role in diminishing the likelihood of conflict escalation. By bolstering transparency and accountability in arms proliferation, nations can actively work towards de-escalating tension and fostering an environment conducive to peace. Embracing multilateral negotiations and cooperative ventures to address security concerns represents a proactive approach to mitigating crises and cultivating enduring peace.

Chapter Ten

Strategic Responses and Recommendations

Analyzing the Strategic Imperatives

Amidst the escalating tensions of the New Cold War, it becomes imperative to analyze and understand the strategic imperatives that can effectively counter threats and stabilize regions afflicted by this global phenomenon. In this pivotal chapter, we comprehensively examine fundamental strategies to address the multifaceted challenges posed by the resurgence of geopolitical strife. The analysis encompasses a wide spectrum of considerations, ranging from military capabilities to diplomatic initiatives, and underscores the critical need for a holistic approach. At the core of this analysis lies the central objective of preserving peace and security while mitigating the increasingly complex risk landscape. Crucially, the strategic imperatives outlined here also underscore the importance of proactive engagement and a forward-looking mindset in averting potential conflict and fostering stability in an uncertain world. As we navigate through these intricacies, it is evident that a nuanced understanding of historical precedents, contemporary power dynamics, and emerging technologies forms the bedrock of effective strategic imperatives. By delving into the nuances of statecraft and international relations, we aim to equip policymakers, analysts, and stakeholders with the necessary insights to craft robust responses and policy frameworks conducive to enhancing global security. By meticulously examining various scenarios and contingencies, we aim to facilitate the development of agile and adaptive strategies that can effectively address specific threats and create pathways for sustainable peace. Ultimately, this analysis aims to underscore the critical nature of strategic foresight and preparedness in navigating the complexities of the evolving global security landscape shaped by the New Cold War.

Enhancing Defense and Military Alliances

In the contemporary geopolitical landscape marked by heightened tensions and strategic complexities, the imperative of enhancing defense and military alliances has assumed paramount significance. With the evolving nature of global threats and the resurgence of power dynamics, nations increasingly realize the necessity of forging robust and collaborative defense partnerships to safeguard their national interests and ensure regional and global security. The efficacy of defense and military alliances lies in their ability to foster collective defense capabilities, deter aggression, and promote a stable international order.

At the core of enhancing defense and military alliances is the principle of interoperability, which underlines the seamless integration of disparate national defense systems and the harmonization of operational methodologies. This requires concerted efforts to standardize protocols, streamline information sharing, and facilitate joint training exercises. By cultivating a cohesive framework for interoperability, allied forces can maximize their combined effectiveness and responsiveness to emerging security challenges, thereby fortifying their deterrent posture and crisis response capabilities.

Moreover, reinforcing defense and military alliances necessitates a calibrated defense investment and modernization approach. Collaborative initiatives aimed at bolstering defense technological capabilities, intelligence-sharing infrastructure, and logistical support mechanisms play a pivotal role in ensuring the agility and potency of allied forces. Strategic coordination in research and development endeavors further enables the creation of cutting-edge defense technologies and innovative operational doctrines, empowering allied nations to confront contemporary security threats with heightened preparedness and resilience.

The evolution of defense and military alliances also demands a holistic consideration of the geopolitical and regional nuances that shape the security landscape. Customized strategic engagements tailored to address specific regional security challenges and asymmetries are instrumental in consolidating the efficacy of alliances. By harnessing a nuanced understanding of regional dynamics, allied nations can proactively address existing fault lines, mitigate potential sources of conflict, and engender a conducive environment for peace and stability.

Additionally, the sustenance and augmentation of defense and military alliances hinge on comprehensive strategic communication and diplomatic engagement. Articulating shared objectives, mutual commitments, and common security imperatives to diverse stakeholders facilitates the consolidation of solidarity and consensus within alliances. Through proactive diplomatic outreach, allied nations can effectively convey their commitment to collective defense, dissuade adversaries from aggressive actions, and engender confidence among partner nations and other stakeholders in the international arena.

In essence, enhancing defense and military alliances represents an indispensable cornerstone of contemporary strategic calculus, offering a potent means to uphold national security, fortify deterrence capabilities, and foster enduring stability. It embodies the strategic imperative of collective security and concerted action in mitigating multifaceted security challenges, thereby epitomizing a proactive and collaborative approach in navigating the intricate contours of the modern security landscape.

Economic Resilience and Self-Sufficiency

In the face of geopolitical tensions and economic warfare, economic resilience and self-sufficiency have gained paramount importance. Nations are taking proactive measures to fortify their economic positions and reduce vulnerabilities to external shocks. This involves diversifying trade relationships, reinforcing domestic industries, and investing in strategic sectors contributing to long-term sustainability. Pursuing economic resilience necessitates a comprehensive approach encompassing fiscal policies, trade arrangements, and investment strategies. Governments are bolstering their national economies through prudent fiscal management, targeted investments in critical infrastructure, and nurturing indigenous innovation and entrepreneurship. Self-sufficiency is a key tenet of this strategy, as it aims to reduce reliance on potentially adversarial nations for essential goods and technologies. Moreover, fostering a robust and diversified economic base enables nations to weather disruptions and challenges, thereby enhancing their overall stability and influence in the global arena. The quest for economic resilience also entails building resilient supply chains, ensuring energy security, and fortifying financial systems against external manipulation. Moreover, governments are increasingly emphasizing the need for agility and adaptability in responding to evolving economic landscapes, including integrating sustainable practices and transformative technologies that enhance environmental stewardship. Collaboration with like-minded partners and regional alliances plays a pivotal role in collectively strengthening economic resilience, creating a network of support and solidarity to mitigate systemic risks and uncertainties. As such, pursuing economic resilience and self-sufficiency constitutes a cornerstone of contemporary statecraft, reflecting the imperative to safeguard national interests and promote sustainable prosperity amidst complex geopolitical dynamics.

Advancements in Cybersecurity Measures

In today's interconnected world, cyber warfare has emerged as a critical battleground where nations seek to gain strategic advantages while defending against sophisticated threats and attacks. As technology continues to evolve at a rapid pace, countries must invest in advanced cybersecurity measures to safeguard their critical infrastructure, sensitive data, and national security interests. Advancing cybersecurity measures necessitates a multi-faceted approach that encompasses technological innovation, intelligence collaboration, and proactive defense strategies.

One key area of focus in enhancing cybersecurity is the development of robust encryption techniques and protocols to secure communication networks and information systems. This involves the continual refinement of encryption algorithms and the deployment of secure communication channels to thwart eavesdropping and data breaches. Additionally, leveraging quantum-resistant cryptography and blockchain technology can further fortify the resilience of digital assets against emerging cyber threats.

Furthermore, implementing sophisticated intrusion detection and prevention systems is vital to cybersecurity readiness. These systems are designed to swiftly identify and mitigate potential cyber intrusions, malware, and targeted attacks, bolstering national defense networks' overall resilience and critical infrastructural facilities. Moreover, integrating artificial intelligence and machine learning algorithms can empower cybersecurity defenses to adapt and respond to evolving attack vectors in real-time.

Collaborative efforts among government agencies, private sector entities, and international partners are essential in tackling the multifaceted challenges of cyber threats. Information sharing and coordinated response mechanisms enable the timely dissemination of threat intelligence, facilitating a unified and proactive approach toward cyber defense and incident response. Additionally, fostering a culture of cybersecurity awareness and education across diverse sectors of society is indispensable in building a resilient cyber ecosystem.

As the threat landscape continues to evolve, the development of offensive cybersecurity capabilities becomes increasingly pertinent to deter adversaries and impose consequences for hostile cyber activities. When executed within legal and ethical frameworks, offensive cyber strategies serve as a deterrent against malicious actors while signaling a nation's resolve to protect its interests in the digital domain.

In conclusion, the relentless pursuit of advancements in cybersecurity measures is paramount in safeguarding national interests and upholding global stability in the face of evolving cyber threats. By leveraging cutting-edge technologies, fostering international cooperation, and cultivating a proactive cybersecurity posture, nations can effectively mitigate the risks posed by cyber warfare and ensure the resilience of their digital infrastructure.

Diplomatic Strategies for De-escalation

Diplomatic strategies for de-escalation are vital in the context of the complex geopolitical landscape presented within the book. With tensions running high and the specter of conflict looming, it becomes imperative to explore diplomatic avenues to defuse the situation and pave the way for peaceful resolution. One key diplomatic strategy involves backchannel diplomacy - discreet and confidential communications between opposing parties facilitated by trusted intermediaries or neutral actors. Providing a less public forum for negotiation allows for more flexible and creative approaches to resolving the crisis without the pressure of public scrutiny. Another crucial approach is the utilization of multilateral diplomacy, leveraging the involvement of various international stakeholders to broker dialogue and negotiations. This not only spreads the responsibility for resolution but also reduces the likelihood of unilateral actions that could exacerbate the situation. Diplomatic efforts should also focus on confidence-building measures to create an atmosphere of trust and reduce hostility between the involved parties. This may involve verifiable commitments to cease hostilities, exchange of prisoners, or establishing communication channels to prevent misunderstandings. Additionally, the deployment of peacekeeping missions under the auspices of international organizations can serve as a tangible demonstration of the commitment to stability and security. Leveraging economic ties and incentives can also be a powerful diplomatic tool. Offering economic benefits or trade concessions in exchange for peaceful cooperation can provide a strong impetus for de-escalation. The careful orchestration of diplomatic overtures, combined with a nuanced understanding of each party's grievances and preferences, is essential for navigating the delicate path towards de-escalation. It requires patience, persistence, and a deep appreciation of the intricate web of political dynamics at play. Ultimately, successful diplomatic strategies for de-escalation demand a delicate balance of assertiveness and empathy, steered by the overarching goal of averting catastrophe and fostering lasting peace.

Legal and International Law Considerations

In the context of the new Cold War and geopolitical tensions, legal and international law considerations play a pivotal role in maintaining stability and preventing escalation. As nations navigate the intricate web of international relations, it becomes imperative to uphold established legal norms and frameworks while adapting to the evolving landscape of global conflict. This section delves into the multifaceted dimensions of legal and international law considerations in the face of contemporary challenges. The foundation of international law, encompassing treaties, conventions, and customary practices, provides the framework for managing inter-state relations. Moreover, the relevance of organizations such as the United Nations and the International Court of Justice cannot be overstated in adjudicating disputes and upholding the principles of international law. In the contemporary context, legal considerations extend beyond traditional warfare to encompass cyber operations, economic sanctions, and influence campaigns. The intersection of law and technological advancements poses unique challenges, raising pertinent questions regarding the applicability of existing legal frameworks in the digital domain. Furthermore, navigating the complexities of sovereignty and jurisdiction in cyberspace necessitates a reevaluation and potential evolution of international law. Additionally, hybrid warfare's ethical and legal implications, which encompasses a blend of conventional, irregular, and cyber warfare strategies, require comprehensive legal analysis and delineation. Adhering to international humanitarian law and human rights standards amidst conflict remains a paramount concern, emphasizing the importance of accountability and the preservation of fundamental rights. Beyond the realm of conflict, legal considerations extend to economic sanctions, trade disputes, and diplomatic negotiations. The intricate interplay between national laws and international agreements underscores the need for coherence and confluence in navigating legal frameworks. Recognizing the nuances of legal pluralism and the diverse interpretations of international law among nations is essential in fostering consensus and mitigating legal discrepancies. In conclusion, adherence to legal and international law considerations serves as a cornerstone for promoting stability, mitigating disputes, and fostering cooperation in an increasingly complex global arena. By engaging in comprehensive legal analysis, nations can navigate the complexities of contemporary conflicts with adherence to established legal norms while seeking adaptability to address emerging challenges.

Public Communication and Information Integrity

In the contemporary landscape of geopolitical conflict, the importance of public communication and information integrity cannot be overstated. This aspect holds critical significance in shaping public perception, influencing policy decisions, and mitigating the spread of misinformation and propaganda. In the New Cold War context, strategic and transparent public communication becomes a foundational element for building trust, garnering support, and countering disinformation campaigns. Many state and non-state actors use sophisticated communication strategies to shape narratives and influence global opinion. It is imperative to establish robust mechanisms for information verification and dissemination to address this challenge. Ensuring the accuracy and reliability of information shared with the public is essential in upholding the integrity of communication channels. The rise of social media and digital platforms has transformed the communication landscape, amplifying the speed and reach of information dissemination. However, it has also presented new challenges, as these platforms can be utilized for the rapid spread of misinformation, manipulation, and propaganda. As such, promoting digital literacy, critical thinking, and media literacy are crucial components of safeguarding information integrity amidst the complexities of the modern information ecosystem. In addition to countering misinformation, effective public communication is pivotal in fostering transparency, accountability, and trust within domestic and international audiences. Governments, international organizations, and relevant stakeholders must prioritize open and honest communication to bridge divides, build consensus, and fortify multilateral cooperation in addressing common challenges. Alongside proactive communication efforts, it is essential to invest in robust cybersecurity measures to protect information integrity from hostile cyber activities. Safeguarding communication infrastructure, combating online threats, and fortifying data protection frameworks are essential components in ensuring the resilience of communication channels. Fostering international collaboration and partnerships to promote information integrity reinforces collective resilience against external efforts to manipulate public perceptions. Building multilateral coalitions dedicated to information integrity upholds the principles of truth, transparency, and ethical communication. Encouraging collaboration among nations, civil society, and private sector entities bolsters the capabilities to combat disinformation campaigns and maintain the integrity of public discourse. In conclusion, prioritizing public communication and information integrity is central to navigating the complexities of the New Cold War. Embracing transparency, countering misinformation, and fostering global collaboration fortify defenses against the weaponization of information and misinformation. By upholding the principles of accuracy, honesty, and responsible communication, stakeholders can mitigate the impact of disinformation and contribute to a more informed and resilient global society.

Building Multilateral Coalition Support

The importance of building multilateral coalition support cannot be overstated in today's complex geopolitical landscape. As nations confront the challenges posed by global security threats, regional conflicts, and transnational issues, the need for collective action and cooperation across borders becomes increasingly evident. This section delves into the nuances of cultivating and sustaining multilateral coalitions to address the multifaceted nature of contemporary security concerns.

Establishing a multilateral coalition involves a deliberate and systematic approach encompassing diplomatic outreach, strategic alignment of interests, and the convergence of policy objectives. At the core of this endeavor lies the recognition that no single nation possesses all the resources, capabilities, or influence required to tackle the array of modern security challenges effectively. Therefore, pooling diverse strengths and expertise through collaborative frameworks is imperative.

Building multilateral coalition support demands meticulous diplomacy, negotiation, and compromise. It encompasses a broad spectrum of initiatives, ranging from bilateral partnerships to broader regional and global alliances. A fundamental principle underpinning such endeavors is emphasizing shared values, common objectives, and mutual trust among participating states. These underpinnings are the bedrock for sustainable, effective cooperation in addressing security challenges.

Furthermore, effective coalition-building rests on cultivating strong interpersonal relationships, institutional linkages, and mechanisms for information sharing. These relationships extend beyond government-to-government interactions, encompassing engagements with non-state actors, civil society, and private sector stakeholders. This inclusive approach widens the scope of collaboration and engenders a sense of ownership and responsibility among diverse segments of society. In doing so, it bolsters the legitimacy and resilience of the coalition as a whole.

Moreover, successful multilateral coalition-building necessitates an acute understanding of the geopolitical dynamics at play and a keen awareness of the aspirations and constraints of potential coalition partners. Each participating nation brings unique geopolitical, economic, and military perspectives, necessitating a balanced approach to negotiations and consensus-building. By acknowledging and accommodating these variations, a coalition can harness the comparative advantages of each member while mitigating potential conflicting interests.

Ultimately, establishing and maintaining multilateral coalition support demands foresight, adaptability, and a long-term perspective. The commitment to nurturing enduring partnerships and fostering a culture of collaboration is critical in navigating the intricate web of global security challenges. Through this cohesive, concerted approach, the international community can fortify its collective resilience and capacity to address the world's multifaceted threats today.

Technological Innovation in Warfare

Rapid technological advancements have redefined the landscape of modern warfare, presenting opportunities and challenges for international security. Integrating artificial intelligence, unmanned systems, and cyberspace capabilities has revolutionized military operations, introducing a new era of hybrid warfare. As nations strive to maintain strategic superiority, investments in technological innovation have become imperative. This section delves into the multifaceted dimensions of technological innovation in warfare, shedding light on its implications.

The proliferation of unmanned aerial vehicles (UAVs) and autonomous weapons systems has significantly transformed combat. With enhanced surveillance capabilities and precision strikes, UAVs have bolstered reconnaissance and tactical advantage on the battlefield. Nevertheless, ethical and legal considerations surrounding autonomous weaponry demand careful attention, as the ethical use of technology remains a critical concern for policymakers and military leaders.

Moreover, cyber warfare has emerged as a dominant force multiplier, enabling states to conduct clandestine operations and disrupt adversaries' critical infrastructure. The integration of offensive and defensive cyber capabilities is pivotal in safeguarding national interests and countering evolving threats in the digital domain. However, the asymmetry and anonymity characterizing cyber attacks pose formidable challenges, underscoring the necessity for robust cybersecurity measures and international cooperation.

Advanced technologies such as hypersonic missiles and directed energy weapons have also garnered significant traction, promising unprecedented speed and precision in engagements. Harnessing these revolutionary technologies demands sustained research and development, fostering collaboration between defense industries, academia, and government entities to uphold strategic deterrence and defense. Nonetheless, the ethical implications of deploying such advanced weaponry present complex moral and legal dilemmas that require careful consideration.

Furthermore, with quantum computing and biotechnological enhancements, warfare paradigms are poised to transform radically in the foreseeable future. Quantum computing empowers states to forge novel encryption methods and optimize military simulations, amplifying their computational supremacy. Meanwhile, breakthroughs in biotechnology raise pertinent questions about the ethical boundaries of genetic engineering and bioweapons proliferation, compelling global communities to establish stringent regulations and oversight mechanisms.

In conclusion, the relentless pursuit of technological innovation in warfare yields profound impacts on international security, necessitating preemptive policy frameworks and guidelines to regulate emerging capabilities' ethical, legal, and strategic dimensions. Decision-makers need to navigate the complexities of these advancements judiciously, prioritizing ethical conduct, humanitarian principles, and collective security imperatives in shaping the future of armed conflict.

Long-term Peace Initiatives

As the specter of conflict looms large in contemporary geopolitics, the imperative for long-term peace initiatives becomes increasingly paramount. Strategic foresight and proactive measures are indispensable in aiming to quell the tumultuous tides of international discord. Long-term peace initiatives should be underpinned by a multi-faceted approach that addresses the underlying root causes of animosity while fostering enduring reconciliation and cooperation. Firstly, diplomatic engagement at the highest levels must cultivate mutual understanding, empathy, and trust among adversarial nations.

This entails sustained dialogue, mediated negotiation, and the cultivation of common ground on which sustainable peace can be erected. Furthermore, intermediary organizations and forums should be leveraged to facilitate constructive communication and peaceful resolution of disputes. Broader peace-building efforts should encompass collaborative ventures in economic development, cultural exchange, and humanitarian aid, thereby nurturing interdependence and shared prosperity. Promoting educational programs and civil society initiatives can also engender a culture of tolerance, inclusivity, and non-violent conflict resolution at grassroots levels. Concurrently, milestones for progress and sustainable peace should be enshrined through legally binding treaties, conventions, and international agreements. These instruments must lay down clear frameworks for dispute resolution, arms control, and protecting fundamental human rights. Moreover, investments in track II diplomacy and people-to-people exchanges play an integral role in fostering enduring relationships and countering political antagonism. Harnessing the power of digital connectivity and social media channels can also serve as conduits for fostering cross-border solidarity and eradicating misconceptions that perpetuate hostilities. Ultimately, long-term peace initiatives necessitate unwavering dedication and patience, recognizing that the seeds of lasting tranquility often take years, if not decades, to flourish. By constructing a unified front of global cooperation to counteract aggression, distrust, and diversion, the vision of sustainable peace can transcend the confines of rhetoric and materialize into a tangible reality, providing a beacon of hope for future generations.

www.ingramcontent.com/pod-product-compliance
Lightning Source LLC
Chambersburg PA
CBHW020355270326
41926CB00007B/435
* 9 7 8 1 7 8 7 9 5 9 7 2 9 *